ON THE ROLLER COASTER CALLED MOTHERHOOD

by
Janene Wolsey Baadsgaard

ON THE ROLLER COASTER CALLED MOTHERHOOD

by
Janene Wolsey Baadsgaard

Copyright © 2004 Janene Wolsey Baadsgaard

All Rights Reserved.

This book is not an official publication of The Church of Jesus Christ of Latter-day Saints.

ISBN: 1-932898-12-3
e. 1

Published by:
Spring Creek Book Company
P.O. Box 50355
Provo, Utah 84605-0355

www.springcreekbooks.com

Cover design © Spring Creek Book Company

Printed in the United States of America
10 9 8 7 6 5 4 3 2 1
Printed on acid-free paper

Library of Congress Cataloging-in-Publication Data
Baadsgaard, Janene Wolsey.
  On the roller coaster called motherhood /
by Janene Wolsey Baadsgaard.
     p. cm.
  ISBN 1-932898-12-3 (pbk. : alk. paper)
 1. Motherhood--Humor. 2. Child rearing--Humor. I. Title.
HQ759.B214 2004
306.874'3--dc22
                                   2004010547

For the dear, universal sister who approached me after I had given a talk at stake women's conference, embraced me with warmth and gusto, then exclaimed with a sigh of relief, "Oh, I'm so glad you're a regular person, just like me!"

CONTENTS

Chapter 1...................................1
A.D. *Always-Diapers Period*

Chapter 2 21
Middle Ages *Unenlightened Period*

Chapter 3.................................39
Renaissance *Renewal Period*

Chapter 4.................................57
Industrial Era *Mediocre Period*

Chapter 5.................................73
The Age of Exploration *Spaced-Out Period*

Chapter 6.................................89
The Age of Reason *Golden Period*

Introduction

It seems that motherhood used to be a lot easier than it is today. Back then, the whole idea was to keep your kids alive and fed for a reasonable length of time. Now our expectations are so high that when our children hit the terrible twos or teens, we mothers feel like total failures.

After my first and less-than-heroic performance in labor and delivery, I sank down in the sheets and peered sheepishly heavenward, sure someone up there was scribbling down an evaluation in red ink: "Subject, Janene Wolsey Baadsgaard, has absolutely no idea what she is doing. Subject will definitely need very intensive remedial work."

Don't get me wrong. I love being a mother, but I'm not very good at it. I'm always afraid I'll be asked to hand in my family history for grading before I get to the happy ending. I'm forever bulging with unborn characters, the plot's still thickening, and we have enough dramatic tension, climax building, and before-dinner hysteria to keep me feeling like a perpetual incompetent.

I just pray that whoever does the grading of that family history doesn't care about commas—or smelly tennis shoes—in the correct place. I hope he accepts rough-draft mothers like me. I hope he gives extra credit for effort and plenty of time for endless corrections and revisions.

But, come to think of it, no one will ever perfect motherhood in this life. Even our perfect heavenly parents have many of their offspring reject their desires for their children's eternal growth. I'm starting to get used to the idea that there will always be pain and elation amid the process of creation, and there will always be an awfully important truth called individual agency.

I now believe we can't learn how to mother from a book, master it like a college degree, plan it like a career, or run it like a business. Motherhood is more like a roller coaster ride during which we're smiling and laughing one minute, then screaming the next. Sometimes, when we find ourselves facing another slow, rickety climb, we wonder why we ever wanted to go on this ride in the first place. Then later we find ourselves wide-eyed in the labor room, paying the fare for another go-around.

These days I like to think of mothering as a high-contact sport. Some players try really hard, some have natural talent, some diligently study the game plan, some wing it—but the only thing you can predict about the mothering game is that you can't predict the outcome.

Once we strap on the belt and that motherhood roller coaster takes off, we're in for the whole ride, willing or not. At some point the truth hits: only when we accept, deep down, that we can't really control everything or anything are we free to embrace the terrifying, wonderful, and exhausting experience. The idea is to hold on tight, take a deep breath, and enjoy the whole wild and unpredictable ride.

CHAPTER 1
FAMILY HISTORY

A.D.
ALWAYS-DIAPERS PERIOD

I have no teeth, my pants are wet,
I will not sleep, my mind is set.
I cry for Mom, I cry for Dad,
When I'm happy, when I'm sad.
They try to feed me mush, and so
I push my lips and let it blow.
It's when they tuck me in at night
They think I'm worth that pretty sight.
I smile and coo and wave to them,
But I'm up again at 2:00 a.m.

Bleep-Bleep-Blurp-Doop

Finding out you're pregnant for the first time is the most life-altering bit of news you will ever receive.

Being pregnant for the first—or even for the seventh time—is really wonderful, except for when it's awful sometimes. But by and large, pregnancy is like being given the privilege of experiencing the magic of Christmas for nine months.

When you find out you're pregnant, it's like being presented a microscopic Christmas present nine months early, neatly wrapped with a don't-open-until sign called a due date. This present continually grows bigger and bigger right under your eyes. You can't peek under the paper or rattle the box, because the contents of this box only rattle from the inside.

Talk about exciting! There you are one day, washing the dishes or scrubbing the toilet, and suddenly you feel something inside you move. Now, you are accustomed to gas bubbles, but this is something different. You immediately stop scrubbing or washing and wait to see if it will happen again. Wow! It happens again.

If anyone is within war whoop range, they know something dramatic has happened. You feel like running outside and dancing in the streets. What you'd really like is to interrupt all regularly scheduled international broadcast programming with a newsbreak live from your kitchen. The reporter would rush in and push a microphone into your face while you stand there in awe, with your scrub brush in hand, and say, "My baby moved. I just felt it move. There was this little blurp and then a bloop-bloop."

This magic moment generally happens after you've spent three long—and I mean long—months continually looking for a place to sleep, racing to the sink just in time, and frantically looking for a bathroom. It's a good thing this monumental event takes place about now, because you've just about had it up to here with being pregnant.

All it takes is that magic bloop or bleep-bleep and you're on cloud nine. Nausea, lightheadedness, continual bathroom emergencies, and extreme exhaustion are suddenly unimportant. There's a real baby in there!

Many people who write about pregnancy are male obstetricians who seem totally oblivious to the truly terrific parts of pregnancy. Even if they go to medical school for eighty-seven years and deliver one zillion babies, men will never have any idea whatsoever how wonderful that first blurp feels.

Obstetricians tend to focus their misdirected attention on making a historical document with copious notes about how much weight you're gaining, but this is a gain that the pregnant one, with whatever grace she can summon, writes off as an acceptable loss. It's all part of the recognition that being pregnant is definitely no piece of cake at times but is pretty wonderful at other times.

D Day

I never thought that finding a place to sit down would be my single goal in life. I never thought that trying to get back up out the chair after I found it would be life's greatest challenge. But being eight months, twenty-nine days, twelve hours, seventeen minutes, and forty-two seconds pregnant can do funny things to a woman.

Some women look great during the last month of pregnancy. I, on the other hand, look as if Michael Jordan just stuffed his favorite basketball into my breadbasket. Being on the short side, I don't do well at hiding the fact that I'm pregnant.

During the last month of pregnancy, all maternity underwear has reached its load limit. With D Day fast approaching, a woman has enough to worry about without being plagued by panty hose that won't stay up and slips that won't stay down.

Pregnant women don't waddle so much because of bulbous middles. Rather, the pregnant waddle is really a juggling act similar to keeping a hula hoop up. First your slip gradually rides up until it forms a solid tire right under your bust line. Then your panty hose gradually ride down until you have to walk funny or sit down and stay there to keep the darn things from zipping down around your ankles and tripping you.

Everywhere you go (actually, you don't go much of anywhere because you can't fit behind the steering wheel and reach the gas pedal at the same time), people ask you the same question—"When are you due?"—as if you're a bomb waiting to go off.

I hate that question. It makes me feel like a giant, unpaid gas bill. I have a due date, all right, but all experienced mothers know that doesn't mean much. It's just a day the doctor or nurse gives you so you won't have to appear stupid when people ask you that dumb question.

But the most difficult thing about being pregnant is that there's only one way out of the situation—and labor and delivery are definitely no strolls in the daffodils. It's either succumb to the inevitable or retain your resemblance to the Goodyear blimp for the rest of your natural life.

The last month of confinement is designed to make women forget what it takes to get it over with. By the time you're big enough and miserable enough to do almost anything, almost anything begins, and you suddenly remember what it takes.

The problem at this point is that there's no turning back. You can't hop off the delivery table, turn to your doctor and husband, and say, "Gee, guys, I think I'll wait till next week to have this baby. I really don't feel like doing this right now."

Most women's first experience in childbirth could be described as unnerving. I, of course, was too dumb to know I was in labor. When I woke at 3:00 a.m. one morning in April, I wasn't alarmed. My baby wasn't due until June. I felt a slight pop and made a quick beeline for the bathroom. My husband and I had spent the entire previous evening guzzling soda pop, and I thought I was paying the consequences for my overindulgence. "Are you all right, Jan?" I heard my husband whisper drowsily from the bed.

"I think so," I reassured him. "But there's water everywhere."

Then it hit. I didn't know what it was, but it made me groan. "What's the matter?" Ross asked again.

"I don't know," I answered, a little more concerned now. But whatever it was, it hurt.

"I'm calling the doctor," Ross insisted, springing up from the bed and dashing for the hall telephone.

"Don't do that. What if it's just too much soda pop, a weak bladder, and a bad gas pain? This is embarrassing," I mumbled.

Ross ignored me and made the call.

"Hello. This Is Ross Baadsgaard. May I please speak to the doctor? Yes, I realize it's the middle of the night, but my wife's just sprung a leak."

By way of excuse here, Ross and I had just started our prenatal classes together, and we hadn't covered water breaking yet. We had passed off breathing exercises like old pros, but we had only attended the first class and still had a little to learn.

"Yes, I'll hold," I heard Ross answer in the telephone. "Yes, doctor. This is Ross Baadsgaard. What do we do now? Yes. I see. Yes sir. We'll be right over."

Then a major contraction hit, and I moaned from the bathroom. Ross hung up the phone and dashed to the bathroom, his eyes wide and still widening.

"The doctor said to come over to the hospital right away. He said it sounds like your water has broken."

"My what?"

"Your water. You know, the water sac the baby's in. The doctor said the chance for infection is great, and I have to get you right over to the hospital, and he'll check on you there."

I suddenly regretted playing Frisbee in the park the night before. I remembered the dirty dishes in the kitchen sink. I thought about my oily hair and threadbare nightgown.

"I have to take a bath first," I answered. "And get dressed and do the dishes."

"You're not doing the dishes. For goodness' sake, Janene, I'm taking you out to the car right now."

"I'm not going anywhere until I have a —" Another contraction. "Moan."

I tried to hold my breath through the pain, then stand up.

"It's impossible," I answered, sitting back down. "I'm leaking all over. I can't go anywhere like this. People will stare at me."

My husband thought for a minute. "I've got it," he said. "You know that disposable diaper they handed out at prenatal class last Tuesday? I'll get that."

"Oh, no!" I answered.

"Wear it," Ross answered, handing me the one and only article of clothing we owned for our little expected one.

He nervously helped me to the car, then charged around to the driver's seat. "How you doing?" he asked as he gunned the engine.

I couldn't answer him. Another contraction was in full force, and I was digging my fingernails into the car seat for support. He sped onto the freeway and headed in the wrong direction. I was absolutely sure my husband was completely turned around and told him so a dozen or more times between moans. He ignored me.

"Do you think we ought to start some breathing exercises?" Ross asked in a rush between stoplights.

He looked over at me. My eyes were bulging out of my head, and I wanted to belt him.

"How can a person be expected to breathe at a time like this?" I finally blurted on a short break between contractions. "That's got to be the dumbest idea anybody ever had."

I don't know how we made it to the hospital, but we did. I sloshed through the emergency room doors and up to the desk.

"Doctor said to bring her over," Ross said in a gush to the nurse at the desk. "Her water's broken."

"Use the elevator on the left and get off on the fifth floor," the nurse said, smiling. "Go to labor and delivery. It'll be on the right once you get off."

As soon as I reached the labor room, a nurse commanded my husband to go back downstairs and check me in. Then she started asking me dumb questions like, "What's your name? What's your doctor's name?"

After about the twenty-seventh question, I sheepishly asked if I could sit down for a minute. She instructed me to lie down on the labor room table, proceeded to check me, then immediately let out a blood-curdling scream. Screaming is not a reassuring thing to do to a first-time pregnant woman.

"You're already crowned!" she screamed as she ran out of room. "Don't push! I've got to get a doctor in here!"

Push what? I thought. I don't want to push anything. I don't think I feel so well.

There I was, crowned with goodness knows what, and both my nurse and my husband had run out on me. There were no cue cards anywhere. What do I do now? I thought. "Heavenly Father," I prayed. "I don't know if I want to do this anymore. I don't know what I'm doing, and everybody else has left me. I'm scared."

A few moments later, a sleepy doctor dragged into the labor room, rubbing his eyes. He began to check me and then suddenly woke up. "Don't push!" he yelled.

"Don't push!" two more nurses chirped. "Pant, like this," the nurse instructed as she raced me down the hallway, banging into the delivery room doors. The other nurse was busy making weird gasping noises for me to imitate. The doctor threw on a gown and gloves, blasted through the delivery doors, skidded across the room, braked just in front of the delivery table, then lunged toward me just in time to catch.

My husband arrived about this time. He looked vaguely like a man from another planet wearing a white space suit. He stepped over to my bed just in time to hear, "It's a girl."

"Can I push now?" I asked from the table.

"Push what?" the nurse answered.

"Look, Jan," Ross said, rubbing my brow with the back of his palm. "Look, it's a baby. Ohhhh, she's beautiful."

The doctor busied himself taking care of a few loose ends, at least earning a little of his fee, while the nurse wrapped my new daughter in a flannel blanket covered with pink and blue teddy bears, then handed her to my husband.

Ross completely melted, one big six-foot-four-inch, two-hundred-pound puddle of butter right there on the delivery room floor.

"Oh, Jan, she's so soft," he whispered.

For the first time in my life, I was speechless.

When the doctor had finished and they had propped me up a little, Ross gently handed me a tiny, warm, pink body, five pounds of a whole, complete person.

When my husband placed my firstborn daughter gently into my waiting arms, I knew. I loved her more than I could contain. I was a mother. I wanted to sing and dance, blow horns and throw confetti, pray and cry.

"Oh, I love you," I whispered. "I love you. I love you."

I kissed her soft, warm, downy forehead and knew instantly what I was made for. Then my newborn daughter opened her eyes, turned her head, and looked up at me.

"Oh, let this be my heaven," I prayed.

I felt more wonder, more majesty, more love than I had ever felt before. And when my husband put his arms around us and enclosed our first small family, I knew I was hooked for life—and then some.

Baby Burps

They say good things come to those who wait. Mothers aren't prejudiced or anything, but they all think their baby is, without a doubt, the most beautiful baby to ever grace this planet.

Babies are, of course, the best idea anyone ever had. With the size of families continually shrinking, I think babies ought to be put on the endangered species list. They need to be protected. Heaven knows what we'd do without them.

There is nothing more awe-inspiring, more promising, than a newborn, minutes after birth, opening her eyes to the light, turning her head to the familiar sound of her mother's voice, opening her tiny mouth for life's first feeding, or loudly wailing at the injustice of it all.

Babies are life's greatest miracle. Even though they go through zillions of diapers and keep you up at night, even though they're continually damp or soggy, babies definitely have their strong points. What else could inspire a normally rational parent to offer lifetime love and free room and board?

Some people will tell you the most endearing sound to a new mother's ears is a coo or a sigh. But all new mothers know that the most comforting sound is a burp.

Basically, what we have here is a very compact person who does not know the difference between night and day. These mixed-up newborn body rhythms help new mothers forget what a good night's sleep is like.

When Baby cries from the crib, he announces feeding time. And with feeding time comes diaper time. It takes a regular professional juggler to keep all spurting areas covered while making a quick diaper change. I never was any good at juggling and had a number of rude middle-of-the-night awakenings.

After an hour or more of feeding and several diaper changes, Mother is definitely ready to put the little one back to bed. Baby, of course, is sleeping soundly and will continue to do so until Mother has crawled back into bed and has almost dozed off. Then comes the "you forgot to burp me" wail, and Mother again rises to the occasion.

New mothers will try any way known to man in order to extract burps. They start with patting and stroking the baby's back. Then they continue into the infant forward-roll technique and progress to tactics like the spread-eagle-over-bouncing-legs maneuver. Nothing works, and Baby is still wailing. It isn't until that lovely burp is finally heard that everyone can rest easy.

Then the moment comes. Baby relaxes into peaceful slumber as the hall clock strikes four, and for a brief moment it seems there is magic in the room. As you sit at the side of the bed, cradling your infant's warm, tiny head in the bend of your neck, you want to hold this moment, to seal it up in some great Kerr jar to open on later lonely nights.

Though you seriously doubt it, especially in the middle of night, you know your bloodshot eyes will clear in time, and your saggy stomach muscles will tighten. But before you're ready for it, there will be no more warm, drowsy heads to cradle, and this time will be gone forever. Though you're tired to the point of exhaustion, you hold your baby closer, trying to embrace it all a little longer.

Doctor, Heal Thine Own Naivete

There's only one thing worse than having a baby with an ear infection—that's having a baby without an ear infection. The scenario goes something like this . . .

Your baby displays all the usual ear infection symptoms, including tugging at ears, loss of appetite, fever, extreme irritability, runny nose, and insomnia.

Red-eyed and exhausted, you decide to call the doctor's office for advice. But all receptionists and nurses give the same advice. "I'm sorry, but we can't tell you what to do until the doctor sees your child in the office."

So what does every dedicated parent do? We take our little less-than-happy bundles to the doctor's office, of course. When our children are most contagious and susceptible to acquiring other infections, we do what every crazy parent does; we take our child to a place where there are more germs concentrated in one small area than anywhere else on the planet—the pediatrician's waiting room.

It seems that every child in the room is either feverish, covered with spots, foaming at the mouth, or coughing blood. But of course doctors are always on schedule. Your wait is likely to last only three or four hours. When you finally hear your name called and you're assigned an examination room, your child has not only his original illness but also has picked up enough other germs to keep him sick for another six years.

By the time the doctor finally gets around to paying you a short visit, your child (who has been screaming with pain in the waiting room for the last four hours, twenty-six minutes, and thirty-eight seconds) suddenly panics and crawls up your face.

Seemingly oblivious to all this, your doctor manages a pleasant introduction and proceeds to de-suction your child from your forehead. Then this helpful healer asks you to help him hold down your child's feet while he braces your child's head against the table. Then he whips out his eardrum flashlight and carefully looks into both of your child's ears. He blows slightly into the little tube that's hooked to the flashlight.

"Your baby's ears look fine," Doctor says, smiling, hoping to relieve your nervous suspicions and send you home happy.

Now what you have is an irritable, ear-tugging, food-refusing, runny-nosed insomniac without an ear infection—and you have a hefty doctor bill.

Doctors are always trying to reassure parents. I think pediatricians have to pass Reassuring Remedial Parents 101 before they can graduate from medical school.

I heard one scholarly professor of pediatrics speak at a parents' seminar the other day. He seriously said, "There is absolutely no reason why a baby should not be a good traveler. It's a matter of attitude. If parents are anxious and expect problems, infants are likely to reflect that anxiety and be fretful as well. Start with the premise that the family will have a good time, and that is what is likely to happen."

This professor failed to mention why new parents are likely be anxious and expect problems. They know that after packing the kitchen sink—along with a few thousand other necessary items like diaper rash ointment, pacifiers, blankets, stroller, bottles, mushy bananas, undershirts, booties, pins, sweaters, bunny suits, bibs, and teething rings—as soon as they get out on the freeway, the baby will need his diaper changed and they'll realize they forgot the diapers.

This professor would have us believe babies spend their traveling hours peacefully sitting in their car seat, dreamily watching the passing scenery and tenderly hugging their teddy. The fact is, most babies devote their conscious traveling hours contemplating ways to destroy their parents' sanity and dismantle their car seats.

This same professor calmly added a sensible precaution to ensure a successful trip: "Be sure the child is in good health to start with. It is not a good idea to travel with a baby who has a fever, rash, or other sign of illness or potential illness."

The professor might have a bit of a credibility challenge here. All experienced parents know that children are coming down with, have, or are just getting over some illness all the time. There may be fifteen minutes during the year when all the children are perfectly healthy at the same time, but that's about it.

Real parents know the truth about being trapped inside a car with one or more of these "good travelers." They try to ignore everything but spurting blood.

This professor also called a fussy baby "fretful." Boy, does he put it mildly. Real babies scream, wail, yell, howl, shriek, roar, bellow, squeal, war whoop, and go into cardiac arrest if their demands are not met in two seconds flat. Real parents try to be patient and calm but never seem to get smart fast enough. I remember a visit to Grandma's house with my good young travelers. When I pulled into Grandma's driveway I vowed like a shell-shocked war survivor, "Never again! Never again!"

Grandma lives in Salem. That's about ten minutes from our home in Spanish Fork.

On Being Three

If you think it's tough being a mother these days, try being a kid. Being three years old is no piece of cake.

Being three means buckles that refuse to unhook when you're desperate for the bathroom; towering people who continually rub the top of your head; and constantly being told, "You'll just have to wait."

Every time you really start having a great time, someone walks in and lectures: "Look at this mess! What in the world are you doing? I just washed those clothes, young man!"

Every time you proudly dress yourself and walk out into the kitchen for your grand morning debut, the whole family snickers.

Your mom looks at your feet and says, "Your shoes are on the wrong feet, dear."

You look down and study your feet and proclaim, "But, Mom, these are the only feet I've got."

When you go to church, your parents make you sit on a hard bench that is so big your legs stick straight out from your hips. You can't see a thing except the bench in front of you. You hear voices up front but haven't the foggiest idea what's being said. Every time you pop up to see what's going on, your parents shove you back down. Every time you make weird noises that send your parents on a laughing spree at home, they scowl at you and blow air through their teeth: "Shhhhhhhhhhh!"

Your parents sit you down firmly every time you start enjoying yourself, and they say things like "If you don't sit still and be a good boy, I'm going to take you out and spank you."

After a while, that spanking looks better than the alternative, but your parents ignore you when you plead, "Please, please, take me out and spank me!"

When you're three, eating can be a real pain. Your wrist tends to lock, your spoon tends to tip in the wrong direction just when you get it to your mouth, and your glass of milk is forever getting in the way of your swinging elbow.

No one takes you seriously when you're three. When you say, "No, I won't eat it—I hate that," they say, "Fine with me, young lady. But just remember—no beets, no apple pie." When you say, "No, I don't want to go to bed," they throw you onto the pillows and promise that if you come out again, you'll be one sorry turkey.

When you say, "I don't want to take a bath," they pick you up and stick your soapy head under the running faucet. When you say, "I don't have to go to the bathroom. I already went last week!" They push you into the bathroom and hold the door shut until you try one more time. It's humiliating.

You can't see what's going on when you're three. But every time you crawl up onto the kitchen counter, your mother yells, "You get down from there before you fall and break your neck!"

Finding play partners is tough, because your mom won't let you leave the yard, cross the street, or talk to strangers. Sometimes even family members are hard to enlist for buddies.

I overheard Jacob, my three-year-old, approaching his eight-year-old brother with a proposition.

"Jordan, will you play with me? Huh? Huh? Huh? Will you be my buddy?"

Jordan turned to him, lowered his eyebrows, and answered, "No! Go away!"

Jacob put his pudgy, jam-smeared hands on his hips and thought for a minute before he shot back, "Well, I guess I'll just my own best buddy all by myself."

Being three teaches you some pretty important lessons. When life gets tough and nobody wants to be your friend, you just have to be your own best buddy all by yourself.

Olympic Galosh Games

Snow brings quiet landscapes, fender benders, and a celebration of the annual Olympic Galosh Games.

Outfitting a young child for cold weather is like trying to put toothpaste back into the tube. No matter how hard you try, he just won't cooperate.

Take the socks, for instance. A child automatically spreads his toes out like a fan when a sock approaches his foot. Try putting a narrow stocking over flared toes. It's no small matter.

Take the pants, for another instance. A child is not like a flamingo. He doesn't know how to balance on one leg without falling over.

"Hold on to my shoulders," you say as you try to help a youngster slip on his breeches.

"No!" is the child's one-word reply to every parental request. Finally this child will lift one leg to slip it inside the pant leg, but he insists on balancing himself without holding on to anything. Down he goes, but not before grabbing his parent's hair, nose, or mouth.

If you're lucky enough to get Junior to hold on to you while you're helping him, you'll soon have your child's foot jammed inside the pant leg. Junior does not know how to point his foot and easily glide it through the pant leg. Children are born with feet permanently stuck in the Egyptian horizontal position.

Where I live, we like to layer our children for cold weather. We start with underwear, proceed to shirts, sweaters, scarves, and several layers of pants and socks. Then we top it all off with the real Olympic feat for feet—getting the boots on.

Putting boots on a young child is like trying to get a fifty-year-old man in and out of his old Army uniform, a large woman in and out of her new girdle, or a teenager in and out of a pair of outgrown blue jeans. What has to fit inside always seems suspiciously bigger than the object it must fit inside of.

Winter is the time of year when all kindergarten teachers deserve gold medals. At least parents have a limited number of boot battles to sweat through.

The last time I was in for a parent-teacher conference, my children's kindergarten teacher looked a bit tired as she told me this story.

"I have seventy students," she related. "There are thirty-five in my morning session and thirty-five in the afternoon. That means one hundred and forty little boots to get back on one hundred and forty big feet."

She sighed before she went on.

"Well, I'd just finished with boots number 137 and 138 on little Billy before I got to the end of the line—your daughter. We shoved and we pushed and we sweated, but we finally managed to get those stubborn boots on her. As I leaned back to take a deep breath, your daughter said, 'These aren't my boots!'

"'Oh, great,' I thought. 'Some fellow student has walked off with the wrong pair of boots.' So we huffed and puffed and pushed and pulled, and finally we got them off.

"Then your daughter sweetly said, 'Those are my big brother's boots, but my mom makes me wear them anyway.'"

Preschool Paranoia

Parents of teenagers get all the sympathy. It seems to be a universally acknowledged fact that teenagers give their parents ulcers. Preschoolers, on the other hand, look so innocent that their parents develop terrible guilt complexes as their sweet little children cause them to question their sanity.

At least when teenagers do something crazy, you can blame it on the transgressor because he's old enough to know better. But just let your two-year-old tap-dance on top of the piano and break the family heirloom rosebud vase with a "one-two-three-kick," and everyone's eyes shift to Mom. "Why did you let him do that?"

ALWAYS-DIAPER PERIOD

It's not that you let him do that, or anything. Preschoolers don't ask for permission. One morning my young son, Jordan, dumped a box of Cheerios on the kitchen floor, then climbed up the stove, sat his wee, diaper-clad bottom on the burner, and proceeded to turn the temperature knob to high.

I quickly took him down and offered him his breakfast. Then he dirtied three bibs, two pair of pants, and five shirts before he threw what food was left onto the floor. The soap he ate while taking his morning bath must have filled him up.

While I was cleaning up his high chair, my little darling raced to the bathroom and threw in a roll of toilet paper and his stuffed musical pig before he flushed.

While I was busy with the plunger in the bathroom, my son raced to the bookshelf, carefully removed a hundred dollars worth of Childcraft books, took the lid off his diaper pail, and threw them in.

While I was trying to iron the crinkled nursery rhyme pages, this child found my sewing basket and became entangled in eighteen colors of thread while he put sixty-eight pins in his mouth, then tried to put his fingers in the fan.

While I was searching for a magnet to retrieve swallowed metal objects, my son climbed up onto the washing machine, turned it on, lifted the lid, and tried to put his foot in the wash cycle.

It's not that I don't try to childproof my home. It just doesn't work. For instance, I took all the books off the bottom shelf of the bookcase when my toddler was big enough to pull himself to a stand and scatter all the books on the floor. That didn't work for long. My baby just kept growing taller, in spite of my advice. Soon the books and knickknacks were moved off the two bottom shelves, then the three bottom shelves. At that point, my toddler waddled down the hall, grabbed his stick horse, then wiped out the entire shelf's contents with a plastic horse head.

When I put the stick horse into the garbage, this same child discovered he could move the front room chair over to the bookcase and climb from the cushion to the arm and then to the back of the chair, where he could, of course, reach his target. When my husband came home and found me threatening to put his child in the garbage, he asked me to think of another alternative.

And what about all those dangerous kitchen cabinets you're supposed to keep the little ones out of? I first tried yelling, "No no!" That didn't work. Next I tried childproof locks. I sure had a hard time getting in and out of my cabinets, but my toddler didn't. He stood guard and ceremoniously watched my husband put a deadbolt lock on one particularly dangerous cabinet. When my husband stood up and turned to put his tools away, this child immediately disengaged the lock, drooled down his chin, smiled, and said, "Look, Da-Da! Open!"

Next I tried putting the most interesting toys in the whole house in a special kitchen drawer just for my toddler. He was told this was his drawer and the others were Mommy's. Now that special toy drawer is the only drawer in the kitchen he won't touch.

If you think keeping toddlers out of the medicine cabinet is tough, try eating a decent meal with them. After the bibs and aprons are tied, the sleeves rolled up, and chairs scooted snugly near the table, you proudly present your young children with a plate full of edibles. The one-year-old will immediately toss his milk across the room and try to stand up in his high chair.

"Sit down," you demand as this child dangles in midair with one foot on the high chair tray, one hand turning the light switch on and off, and the other hand dragging the phone through his potatoes.

At this point, the three-year-old will pull off his bib because it "itches his neck"—right before he proceeds to dump an entire bowl of tomato soup down his white shirt. And the four-year-old starts giggling, and the one-year-old finally sits down—in his beets. The two-year-old is stuffing green peas up her nose.

My husband suggested we put a drain in the center of the kitchen floor and tile everything, like they do in the public showers. He said we could dress the kids in raincoats when they eat, then simply bring in the garden hose and let them have it after every meal.

I have been known to pick up my dinner plate, head down the hall, and lock myself inside the only private room in the house. The only peaceful meal I've enjoyed in ages was the time I sat in the bathroom with my dinner plate on the hamper, running water full blast in the sink so I couldn't hear what the kids were throwing in the kitchen.

For Lack of Love and Attention

After the birth of my sixth child, a well-meaning friend asked, "Well, don't you think it's time to have a little break between babies?"

I was feeling overwhelmed at the time and agreed with her suggestion. After getting home from the hospital and facing life alone with my young children, I often found myself wondering at the end of the day if I could possibly give my children everything they needed.

It seemed there was so much time taken up with manual tasks—like washing dishes, clothes, walls, faces, fingers, and toes—that very little time was left over for the things I felt were much more important, like time to be alone with each child and talk, time to tell stories or play games.

As I looked at my beautiful six-month-old baby, it seemed as he had gone from a tiny, newborn infant to a wiggly, bubble-blowing baby without my even noticing. I longed for the hours I had spent with my first child. I wanted those hours to rock and cuddle and fall asleep together. I wanted those hours for one-to-one sharing.

I wondered about our decision to have our children while we were young and raise them close together. As I folded the clothes, I watched my baby on the floor as he grabbed at his toes and tried to stuff them in his mouth. I knew it would only seem like moments before he would be crawling and then running and screaming with his brothers and sisters. I wondered if my baby would suffer from lack of individual time and attention.

Just then my two-year-old son ran into the room. As soon as he saw his little brother, he ran toward him, lay his head on his back, and patted his bottom. Then he jumped up, ran and grabbed his favorite tattered blanket, and covered him gently. Then my three-year-old daughter came into the room. When she saw her little brother on the floor, she immediately lay down next to him. The baby turned his face to her and smiled and cooed as she smothered his face with kisses and said, "Oh, you cute little button. I love you. You're my favorite buddy."

Then my seven-year-old daughter came into the room and sat the baby up on the blanket. She lifted him to his feet and they rubbed noses.

Then my five-year-old son came into the room and said, "Hey, it's my turn to play with Jacob. You always hog up too much time."

Then my eight-year-old daughter walked into the room and promised she'd do the seven-year-old's dinner dishes if she let her rock Jacob. She picked up the baby and carried him to the oversized rocker.

The two-year-old ran and grabbed the baby's pacifier and popped it into his mouth while the rest of them snuggled together on the rocker. My five-year-old spread his blanket over everyone's knees after he crawled to the chair to join the others.

My seven-year-old picked up a book and started to read to a quiet audience. "Once upon a time," she began.

That baby is suffering from lack of attention and love? I thought as I finished mating the last sock and headed toward the kitchen sink to do a pile of dishes.

Slowly my self-doubts melted as I watched my children together in the rocker they had so appropriately named our "love seat."

CHAPTER 2
FAMILY HISTORY
MIDDLE AGES
UNENLIGHTENED PERIOD

When Mommy sent me off to school,
I thought I would forget the rules.
Then if I had to go—what then?
If I had—oops—already been?
What if I get my papers wrong?
What if I do not know the song?
What if the lunch bell is too late?
What do I do if I can't wait?
What if my zipper just gets stuck?
What if my teacher says, "Tough luck!"
Mom . . . I don't feel too well
When I hear that loud school bell.

Ready for School

When kids are in school, mothers everywhere are faced with the same problem. It's one major obstacle course to get all those bodies bathed, dressed, combed, fed, and out of the door before the tardy bell rings. All this is difficult, but not life-threatening. It is what comes next that brings every mother to her knees.

After you get all the eating, dressing, and combing done and you're ready to take a deep breath because it's only seventeen seconds before the bus comes, every child remembers at precisely the same instant what he had forgotten. You are suddenly bombarded with:

"Mom, you need to sign my reading chart."

"Mom, what does the rotation of the earth have to do with the climatic conditions around the world? Quick, it's going to be on my geography test this morning."

"Mom, it's my show and tell today, and teacher said I can't bring any more things that breathe unless you come with me and take it back home with you." (The sack rattles.) "It's breathing, Mom."

"Mom, I can't find my: (a) piano book, (b) other shoe, (c) underwear, (d) gym shorts, (e) glue, (f) backpack, (g) library book, (h) eraser, (i) locker combination, (j) newspaper article, (k) coat, (1) boot, (m) jacket, (n) umbrella, (o) book report, (p) tissue [Yes, tissue. The whole mob of my children's teachers request a box of tissue each year.], (q) Weekly Reader money, (r) high school play money, (s) field trip money, (t) book club money, (u) school picture packet money, (v) lunch money, (w) reading calendar, (x) pencil box, (y) lunch pass, or (z) insect collection."

Of course, by now mother can't find her: (a) sense of humor, (b) sanity, or (c) patience.

Some day, I tell myself, I will rip off my ratty housecoat, fuzzy slippers, and morning breath, then make a quick change into fluorescent leotards. Instantaneously I will become a supermom who arises at 4:00 a.m., and showers, dresses, styles her hair, and puts on her makeup by 4:03. I will play classical music as I breeze about the kitchen flipping eggs and squeezing fresh orange juice while my children wake and happily go about doing their morning chores. Later we will have a well-planned, unhurried family devotional to give everyone the perfect start to their well-planned, unhurried day. Maybe things would go a little smoother if I approached my mornings this way.

But one of these days never seems to come, and I find myself dragging out of bed at the last possible moment. Before I step into the shower, I yell my standard, tender, motherly good morning greeting to my children: "You kids turn off that TV before it pickles your brain."

Mornings don't always run smoothly around my house. We're like a pack of nervous thoroughbred horses before the race begins. But before any nervous filly or colt leaves my starting gate, this old mare gives them a juicy kiss and hug big enough to last through the scraped knee at morning recess, the cardboard lunch at noon, and the failed math test in the afternoon.

My children are not always dressed in matched clothing, but I hope they're dressed in the assurance that no matter how tough it gets out there, someone who loves them will always be here when they come home. And I don't even think it will matter to them if that someone is wearing fluorescent leotards or a ratty housecoat and fuzzy slippers.

Raggedy Underwear

When you're born into a family, you're assigned a lifetime position. Forever after you will either be the big kid, the middle kid, or the baby. It doesn't matter how old you get in real life, birth order assignments stick forever.

The big kids are the ones who get all the new clothes and lots of attention because Mom and Dad were always feeling guilty that they forced them to grow up too fast with too many younger siblings coming up through the ranks too soon. They are the ones who "are old enough to know better" whenever something goes wrong. When they get married, they have to rent a U-Haul to cart off their photo albums of baby pictures.

Big kids like to be in charge and tell their brothers and sisters when to jump and how high. But eventually they get all the blame when something goes wrong because they were in charge and should have made the other kids stop it before the table cracked.

The middle kids are the ones who spend their entire childhood wearing the big kids' old, worn-out, raggedy underwear. When you're a middle kid, you're too little to "stay out that late," and too big to "act like that." I always thought being in the middle of my family gave me the best view. I was able to watch my older brother and sisters struggle through amateur parents, pimples, dates, and drivers' licenses before it was my turn, along with watching my younger sisters race through diapers, trikes, and kindergarten. Everything in between, I was in the middle of.

Middle kids have a tendency to get lost in the sibling crowd, so they go to great lengths to dream up ways to get a little attention. This rarely works, however. I ran away for a day once and nobody even noticed.

The little kids get lots of attention because they signal the end of the train and everybody loves the caboose best. I've never figured out whether they like the caboose best because it's so cute or because it's finally the end of the train. The little kids get new clothes and underwear like the big kids because all old clothes first go to the middle kids, then to the rag box. The little kids can never, ever, not in a million years and with two Ph.D.'s, know as much as the big kids.

Growing up with a bunch of kids does have its advantages. My family of origin avoided a lot of typical problems because of sheer numbers. For instance, we never had any eating problems in my family. By the time we had each received our share of the food, the portion was so small and we had waited so long for our turn that we'd eat anything.

Children in large families seldom develop guilt complexes. When Mom shouts, "Who ate all the chocolate cake?" Nobody has to feel guilty or even own up, because they know they've seen at least three or four of the other kids sneak a piece down to their bedrooms after they did.

Children in large families never get a chance to feel bored or lonely. Whenever someone makes a suggestion like "Anybody want to play basketball?" there is an instant game with enough people to play on both teams.

Keeping the house clean in large families is uncomplicated too. When the doorbell rings, each child simply grabs an armful of clutter and mess and throws it behind the couch. Even dishes aren't too complicated. There is usually at least one child for every day of the week who is assigned dishes. Getting everybody to take his turn is a little more difficult.

Picking out friends for bridesmaids at weddings is never a problem, either. My husband has seven sisters and I have seven sisters. That made fourteen bridesmaids. Who had room for friends?

Even though families mean delights and frustrations, crowded station wagons and bathrooms, kids should have the adventure of growing up in the safe harbor called home. And if they're lucky, they'll know the blessings and blunders of many brothers and sisters.

The Great Family Getaway

I love vacation season—when I'm safe at home. Because I live near the mouth of Spanish Fork Canyon, I have ample opportunity to spy on family vacation caravans headed into and out of the canyon for their annual safari into the unknown.

Campers, trailers, and overloaded station wagons speed into the canyon full of clean, excited families ready for the great escape. Outfits leaving the canyon are a different story. Vehicles on their way home are covered with mud, burning oil, and all seem to be dragging their exhaust pipes. (Families typically bring home more than they start with.)

Family vacations would be a lot easier if not for the criminal offender every family seems to produce. This family culprit insists on bringing home mountains of mementos.

My mother was the classic vacation rock collector. Everywhere we traveled she would load another rock into the trunk to remind us of the places we'd been. While we were edging up a steep mountain pass on one vacation, the family station wagon kept stalling. With each stall my dad would run around to the back of the car and throw out one of Mom's rocks. This pattern repeated itself for miles as we tried to reach the summit. By the time we finally reached the top of the mountain, all the souvenir rocks had been tossed. I was sitting in the back seat, absolutely sure my dad would try tossing out kids when he ran out of rocks.

Mother must have shared her passion for vacation souvenirs with me. In a few short years, I developed into the classic child collector of animal relics. I had my sights set on starting a natural history museum under my bed.

I thought I was being pretty sneaky as I tucked the seashells, bird nests, frogs, and horned toad into my suitcase beneath my underwear. But my family always got wise to my carry-home companions after the air conditioner invariably broke down and the temperature in the car topped a hundred degrees. Weird dead-animal smells seeped through the crack in my suitcase in a green mist.

Vacations without at least one wacky souvenir collector would be less weird and smelly. But I have a feeling they would be pretty boring. Ah, what any parent would give for even one moment of boring on a family vacation! We spend all year looking forward to the annual family vacation because we have grown senile and forgotten last year. The major problem with a family vacation is that you have to take the family along.

Family vacations would be a lot more fun if you didn't have to get into a car and drive there with all the children within three feet of you. I'm not complaining, but I have finally decided family car designers must be either naive and childless or a bunch of parental nitwits with chronic smart-loss.

Climbing inside a family vehicle with living, breathing children for any length of time is like being pushed into a prison cell at the local penitentiary (but even maximum security cells come equipped with sanitary facilities). Once you close that car door and start the ignition, you are definitely trapped until you've paid your price to society for bringing these unruly wild animals into the world.

Whatever anyone yells, you have to listen to. Whatever anyone does to stink up the car, you have to smell. Whatever anyone throws, you either wipe up later, or get hit in the head with immediately.

What family cars really need are bulletproof, soundproof windows such as the police cars use when they transport dangerous criminals. I can see it now. My husband and I are sitting alone in the front seat of the car, speeding happily down vacation highway. There is brutal fighting in the rear of the car; we cannot hear it. There is car sickness; we cannot smell it. There is bomb throwing; we do not get hit. It would be heaven!

Eventually our wild wrestlers would probably get tired and a little desperate for parental attention. I can picture their next move. Way too many mouths and noses are mashed against the bulletproof window, drooling, dozens of fingers clawing at the glass. But we are totally oblivious as our peripheral vision feigns child blindness. I will be clipping my toenails and giving my husband cheerful directions from the road map while he is singing, "Oh, give me a home..."

If the kids are lucky we may turn, smile, and wave every hundred miles or so.

Campout Chaos

The canyons are plumb full of crazy people in the summer. Now, these people are pretty sane at other times, but throw them a hot summer weekend after a long work week and they suddenly take flight and rush to the closest available mountains.

These people enjoy running water, modern appliances, and indoor plumbing at home, but they throw it all away for the annual primeval ritual, the family campout.

Our family campout team usually consists of one or two well-intentioned parents and way too many ill-intentioned children. Well-intentioned parents want their children to enjoy God's magnificent creations, breathe fresh mountain air, dip their toes in clear mountain streams, run with majestic deer, and smell the wildflowers. Ill-intentioned children, on the other hand, plan creative ways to drop their entire dinner in the campfire, touch the poison ivy, dismantle the tent, fall over cliffs, poke sticks at rattlesnakes, and cause it to rain for six straight days.

A family campout requires a great deal of planning. One Friday night after a rotten week you get an insane impulse, throw a couple of sleeping bags and kids in the back of the car, and take off for the hills without even thinking about the consequences. You leave the smog, congestion, heat, and crowds of people behind, right? Wrong. There are always a few hundred million people with the same idea on precisely the same weekend. The campgrounds are full of insomniac, deaf teenagers with ghetto blasters, gathered for all-night parties.

By the time you finally set up camp, the kids are starving and the temperature dips. Then you realize you forgot your jackets and matches. Later, even your Boy Scout training doesn't come in handy when you can't go to sleep because the ground is harder than day-old baby mush. You're in for the longest night of your life.

My family recently spent a night in the mountains. We watched the sun's pattern of light and dark on the quaking aspen, saw deer leaping through the meadows, and listened to the wind in the pines.

We also had several children who had to go real bad but refused to do so in the dark, got bitten by mosquitoes, and ate black-charred hot dogs and marshmallows. Pregnant and nauseated, I spent the longest sleepless night of my life trying to get comfortable with all of us in one small tent. I was never so happy to see the morning light and know our wonderful wilderness experience was about to come to an end.

The family campout makes our smoggy, crowded neighborhoods look like heaven. I find myself bowing before my bathroom door with new respect and being dumbfounded at the miracle of a hot shower. My lumpy old mattress never looked so good.

Springtime Arrives on the Bottom of Tennis Shoes

I can always tell when spring is just around the corner.

No, I can't tell because some chubby little groundhog told me so or because the tulips are breaking through the soil in the flower bed. I know spring is in the air when I start spending my romantic evenings scraping mud off my children's tennis shoes. The outside entrances to my home are in a state of constant open. Little black dots on my kitchen window hatch into flies, and my husband tries out the new tent in the living room.

I'm never ready for this.

While everybody else is outside frolicking in the sunshine, I'm loading another batch of smelly clothes into the washer.

My husband seriously told me I shouldn't let the children play on the grass this time of year. Can you believe that?

"If you let the kids play on the grass when it's wet like this," he said, "it will mat the grass down and kill it."

"Just think," I answered. "No lawn. No mowing, fertilizing, dragging leaky hoses all over the yard . . ."

He smirked, then left for work.

Just try sending your kids outside to play on one small grass-covered backyard without a patio. Then yell the strict instructions, "Now, you kids stay off the grass."

Of course, once you get the kids out of your hair and outside to play, you get them coming and going from all outside entrances looking for drinks, bathrooms (in that order), toys, snacks, and referees.

"If you go out, stay out," I find myself yelling. "Of course, if you want to come back in the house, I do need someone to clean the bathrooms."

This last comment always helps my kids decide whether to stay in or go out.

But even with all its misgivings, springtime and children are the perfect mix. "Hey, Mom!" my three-year-old son exclaimed excitedly one morning after a few moments alone in the backyard, "It's springin' all over out there!" And it was. Little sprigs of new growth were circling out from barren limbs of trees everywhere.

Brown, lifeless grass was slowly turning a brilliant shade of green. Birds reappeared. The whole earth seemed to smell of newness, evaporating the winter death of cold and darkness.

My young children are the springtime in my life. To them, everything is new and fresh, a singularly new experience. They feel deeply the wonder of life I've allowed to slip away. So, seeing the void inside myself, I hurry to rediscover the world with them.

Having children is like being granted the once-in-a-lifetime privilege of being a child again. For now you follow behind, while a small one takes the lead and introduces you to your world again.

UNENLIGHTENED PERIOD

Family Home Evening Enigma

Parents have been promised great results if they will hold regular family home evenings. Since most mothers will be asked to pass this endurance test, it may be helpful to know how this should be done.

First, try to locate all of your children sometime Monday evening. A 33 percent attendance average may be all right for church, but it is not acceptable for the home front. Next, clear your throat and try to sound pleasant when you cup your hands around your mouth and yell, "You kids get in here right now! It's time for family night."

If no one appears in the next forty-seven minutes, more drastic measures are needed. Ignore what your children say as you drag them from their televisions, headphones, and radios. Next, sit firmly in your favorite living room chair and wait for your husband to call the family to order. There are times when a Mormon family home evening might be compared to a funeral, in the sense that you have an uncomfortable gathering of family members who would rather be somewhere else. The major difference is that at a funeral someone has died.

During more trying family home evenings, although no one dies, everyone's sense of humor sure does. A normally warm, loving family gathering can become a regular Japanese wrestling match, only we usually wear more clothes.

Fathers are generally required to preside at these weekly functions. At any other church meeting where Father presides, his underlings respectfully give him their undivided attention. Sometimes family home evenings are not the same. It's next to impossible to get everybody quiet at any given time. If the decibel level fails to lower to a dull roar, fathers generally turn the meeting over to—you guessed it—Mother.

Singing "Welcome to Family Night" while you tap out a soft-shoe routine and balance the new china on your head may get everyone's attention, but don't count on it. Most likely, Johnny will be too busy bugging the heck out of Susie, Mike will be cleaning out the dirt between his toes, and your teenage daughter will be too interested in the novel she's hiding under a couch cushion. But of course, your husband will be grinning.

Now, pretend you are still in charge, then turn the meeting over to your husband, who turns it over to the four-year-old, who is always in charge, anyway, and has an opening song prepared.

This budding music apprentice will most likely bonk every family member on the head with his baton, then proceed to sing a solo with seventeen verses. Or he will suddenly get in the mood to favor the whole family with a piano solo which consists of hitting every single key on the piano 867 times.

At this point it is too late for medication. Family planning councils are great to insert here. This is when you plan your week as a family so members can support one another. This is also when you find out that the high council meeting, Young Women's planning meeting, Primary party, Bears' den meeting, ward temple day, and stake high priests social have all been scheduled for Tuesday at precisely 7:00 p.m.

Prayers are wonderful in family home evening, especially when they are the closing kind. Younger members tend to offer short, blessed, to-the-point prayers like "Heavenly Father, thank thee . . . all the way. Amen!"

Ask the four-year-old to say the closing prayer after an especially tiring meeting.

As children get older, of course, their prayers get more mature. They progress to things like, "And please bless my brother J-A-S-O-N [spelled to avoid any confusion] to quit hitting me and taking my candy and . . . Ouch! . . . Dad . . . Jason's pinching me . . . and bless Grandma and . . . Hey! Jeffery's peeking . . . I'm not going to keep praying when there's someone peeking. . ."

When it comes right down to it, there are basically two kinds of family home evenings. Those with great refreshments and those without. Those with, are better.

But the better part of family home evening has a way of sneaking up on you. It happens when you forget you're doing your duty and start discovering what's happening around you. Your toddlers may still be spinning cartwheels off the armchair, but you actually start feeling warm inside as you let your hair down, slide off the sofa, and sit cross-legged on the floor.

You suddenly realize no one is watching or taking minutes or preparing the monthly report for a stake president on this meeting. You can do family home evening your way. And there are times when all the effort really starts to pay off. You may watch your twelve-year-old conduct the meeting like an old pro or your seven-year-old give a lesson that sort of chokes you up. Maybe no one can guess that you're a toad sunning on a rock while you're playing charades, but your whole family starts to seem pretty great.

Being together as a family may not always be peaceful, but it is life on this planet at its core. Children's voices may more often sound like shrieks than songs, but somewhere behind that noise is one universal voice that swells to sing: "I want to grow. I want to know. I want to be. I want to see." Families give you a place to do all that.

When one man truly loves one woman, the family they create can change the whole world and make it new again. That's where kingdoms start. There is no greater miracle. There is no better place to learn of trust and communication, caring and sharing, life and love.

Like the ocean, family life is often full of conflict and change, but there are times when the billowing tempest ends, the swelling calms. When we look out over the vastness of the seas, the horizon seems distant and impossible. And even with our ship headed toward the light at the end of vision, the horizon fades forever and forever forward as we move. But the truest joy comes during the journey, not at some imagined perfect port. There is no perfect family. But lasting joy does come as we experience life face-to-face and arm-in-arm with our fellow crew members.

Thanks, Jacob, I Needed That

My family does our best to keep this old planet from spinning off its axis. Each week we have a planning session which consists mainly of Mom standing next to a giant paper calendar taped to the refrigerator while each family member yells out what they have on their agenda for the week.

Now, don't get me wrong, we are not one of those boring Franklin families who try to give their children a day planner on their first birthday. This is our way of staying in touch with each other, our feeble attempt to make some sense and order out of our hectic lives.

I'm telling you this because a while back something happened to change my idea about sense and order. While I was busy writing up my husband's meetings on the calendar, my five-year-old son quietly tiptoed to my side and whispered, "Mom, on Tuesday write, 'Jacob has to do ... nothing.'" I wasn't paying attention and he repeated a little louder, "Mom, on Tuesday write, 'Jacob has to do ... nothing.'"

When Jacob gets something on his mind, I've found it's much easier to do what he says than pay the consequences. So instead of reasoning with him about the silliness of taking up limited calendar space, I quickly wrote exactly what he said in minute script on the corner of the square marked Tuesday. Jacob liked the look and power of his new plans and continued in his boss-to-secretary voice, "On Wednesday write, 'Jacob has to play with friends, goof off, and have fun.'"

I began dutifully taking his dictation for Wednesday, then stopped. "Now Jacob, we're trying to do our family planning for this week. Don't interrupt me any more," I said before Jacob could quite complete his further instructions for Thursday.

Well, we finished our planning session, the clean white numbered squares quickly filling up with commitments for every day of the week. Later we dashed into our bedtime bustle routine.

It wasn't until after breakfast the next morning that I glanced over at the calendar on the refrigerator and began reading the mass of activities that would fill my family's week. I felt like crawling back into bed and pulling the blankets over my head. Juggling the demands and commitments of twelve people is no small matter. Then I noticed that tiny notation in the upper corner of the square marked Tuesday: "Jacob has to do . . . nothing." Jacob's plans suddenly looked pretty good.

I wondered if maybe we'd all be better off if we carefully pulled out our leather-bound day planners and efficiently wrote in the square reserved for Tuesday, 'Janene (you can fill in your own name here) has to do . . . nothing." And I think we'd all feel a little less tired if we regularly wrote in the square marked Wednesday, "Have to play with friends, goof off, and have fun."

I know, I know—somebody has to make a living and fix supper. But the problem is we start filling up our lives with so many shoulds and oughts, we sometimes forget we don't really have to do anything. What we do is by choice. I'm not sure I'm ready to accept that fact, but truth it remains. We don't have to do anything. We choose to live as we live, and if we don't like it, we can stop and shout, "Hey! Hold it! I want to rethink this for a minute."

After all the thinking is over and all the shoulds and oughts are pushed aside for a time, I think a lot of us would actually just pick up where we left off and keep doing what we were doing all along. Only this time we'd do it with a new twist. We'd now live as we live not because we have to but because we choose to.

Thanks, Jacob. I needed that.

Beautiful Noise

The hours following the evening meal definitely separate the men from the boys.

After supper, parents dream of soft sofas, quiet reading, or a little romantic music. Children, on the other hand, use the evening meal as a frantic pit stop to refuel for the rest of the high-speed race until bedtime.

It's enough to make even the most patient parent contemplate repeating the well-known solution found by the old woman who lived in a shoe. I've never believed those nursery rhyme illustrations that show her with ninety-seven hair-raising kids. Nobody has that many kids. She probably had five or six, but after supper, they suddenly became "so many children she didn't know what to do."

The other evening, after a hectic dinner hour, I retreated to the love seat for a few moments of peace and leisurely newspaper reading. The children had other things in mind. Aubrey began practicing her shooting technique with a plastic suction basketball hoop she planted on my forehead. Arianne, Joseph, and Jacob created hurricane force winds racing around me, while big brother Jordan and big sister April played stick-out-your-foot-and-watch-little-brothers-and-sister-trip.

At this point, I was about to yell something unprintable when I decided instead to count to ten. Gradually my pulse slowed, the red left my neck, and I began listening to a strangely beautiful noise around me.

All the family chaos seemed to transform into myriad musicians warming up before a concert begins. I began to see quiet purpose in the nerve-racking finger exercises and disquieting disharmony. I realized it takes time to fine-tune the instruments—and, more important, minutes, hours, days, weeks, and years of difficult practice before a musician ever reaches the concert hall.

Budding musicians need time, lots of time, before they're ready to hear the unique melody only they can play. All this preparation called home and family life leads to something wonderful.

It takes all kinds of instruments—the gentle, steady strings, the rebellious brass, the unpredictable percussion, and the mellow woodwinds—to make the orchestral family complete, to create a deep, resonating, bright, full expression of sound.

It takes all kinds of individuals to make the rich, living music of families. There is no right or wrong song or more important rhythm. There is only vibrancy in variation and excitement in individual expression. The most beautiful family score is a true mosaic of the air, an invisible voice of creation.

As a parent, I hope maybe somewhere along the way I may have inspired a note or two or penned a few choice lyrics in my children. But when the concert begins, I know my child will be on his own.

When the musicians carefully position their instruments, then raise their eyes to the master to begin, I will be on the front row—my child's most devoted fan as he singularly follows the music he hears, his joyous solo amidst the symphony of life.

CHAPTER 3

FAMILY HISTORY

RENAISSANCE
RENEWAL PERIOD

My hands are pricked with sewing pins,
I don't know which week I'm in.
My two-year-old has lost her shoe,
My eight-year-old has got the flu,
My missionary's getting thin,
My daughter won't claim me as kin.
The dog just threw up on the rug.
The sink's stopped up, I think it's plugged.
My hair's a mess, my socks all run.
I ask, "Now am I having fun?"
Sometimes I think I'm going mad—
Then the holidays don't seem so bad!

A Valentine Between the Pickles

Hi there, you good-looking hunk of a man. This is your wife speaking. (I know this valentine may come as a bit of a surprise, since I'm putting it between the lettuce and mustard on the bologna sandwich I'm packing for your lunch. But I just wanted to make sure you were paying attention.)

I wanted you to know...

I used to love you for the way you looked in your football uniform. Now I love you for the way you look in your PJs after you've been up with the sick baby all night.

I used to love your muscles, strong from lifting weights in the gym. Now I love your muscles best when they're used for carrying loads of laundry to the washing machine, Jordan to the roof for his sixty-seventh lost softball, Jacob when he's too tired to walk any more at Disneyland, and me to the car after I lost too much blood in the emergency room.

I used to love you for taking me out to expensive restaurants. Now I love you for making Postum and cinnamon toast for me to eat while we watch the ten o'clock news.

I used to admire the way you washed and waxed your sports car. Now I admire the way you wash and wax our babies' behinds at bath time and the way you always carefully polish each individual apple with the kitchen towel before you fill the Christmas stockings.

I used to admire your latest intellectual recital from your vast store of knowledge. But now I admire you when you are on all fours, acting like a goon to get the baby to laugh, or attentively listening to our preschoolers tell knock-knock jokes without punch lines.

I used to love you for romantically lighting up my life. Now I love you for magically focusing my life when you find my glasses, or lighting up the children's lives by pretending to turn on the car lights just by touching your nose.

I used to admire your courage to travel to exotic foreign lands. Now I admire your courage to stay home and get up every morning, face the work world, then come back home to sticky kitchen chairs and floors, smelly tennis shoes, peanut butter and jam dinners, and, after dinner, children who explode with "Daddy-do-this" energy.

You are my husband and my sweetheart, but you are also the father of my children. You spend your free time fixing flat bicycle tires, putting up swings in the backyard, building clubhouses—and your children's memories.

You are not the same man you were before we were married. You may have a few extra pounds and a little less hair, but you're the only handsome hunk for me. You are my lover and my best friend.

If I love you this much more now than I loved you then, just think what we'll feel like eighty-four zillion years from now.

Years ago we knelt across an altar gazing into each other's eyes, believing our love was complete. Now we gaze across a crumpled bed at 6:00 a.m. with one child crawling across your stomach, another perched on your nose, one ready for a jet landing on your shins, and one nestled in the crook of your arm. The others are spilling Cheerios in the kitchen.

I love you, honey. Happy Valentine's Day, Dad.

When It's Easter at the Baadsgaards'

My husband brought home two rabbits for the children last Easter.

"The black lop-ear is a male, and the white dwarf is a female," he said nonchalantly.

I dropped my jaw to China. "Dear, don't you know what that means?"

"1 think it will be a 'good experience' for the kids," he answered. "You know, seeing how baby bunnies get here."

I shook my head. You'd think realizing how all our baby Baadsgaards got here would be enough for any man.

Months of child-in-company-with-rabbit heaven passed quickly, with much backyard romping and garden raiding. I was beginning to think maybe my husband was right. The whole family loved our newest members and wanted to learn everything we could about raising them. We haunted the library, and my husband picked up a booklet he mistakenly thought contained good rabbit-raising information.

The children turned white when they read the booklet, and it turned out to be a giant collection of lavish rabbit recipes, complete with full-color main course pictures and expert pelting techniques. They wouldn't speak to their father for days.

My husband felt terrible. He ceremoniously threw the booklet into the trash, lined the children into a fire detail, and quickly reenacted the book-burning crimes of yesteryear. But when the inevitable finally happened, even my husband was not mentally prepared for the abundance of our "good experience."

"Dad and Mom!" our young son bellowed, slamming through the back door. 'There's something moving in the straw!"

My husband smiled, stood proudly, adjusted his pants, and left to inspect his carefully orchestrated "good experience." He held back the stampede of berserk, screaming children by whispering, "Now kids, new mothers tend to be nervous. If you make Scamper nervous, she's liable to eat the babies or something."

With that mental image flashing through their brains, the kids quieted down and silently followed their father out to the rabbit hutch.

"There's two little baby bunnies out there," my son yelled to me as my proud husband and the kids returned. "A black one and a white one, just like Scamper and Renaldo."

Each day following our first discovery of maternal delight, my husband and the kids made it a daily morning ritual to check on the bunnies. On the second day, my husband returned to the house and announced, "Why, there's three bunnies, not two."

On the third day, he announced, "My land, there's four babies out there."

The next day he walked through the door a little slower and announced, "Jan, I think she's given birth to six."

On day five, he walked through the door with a glazed look in his eyes and simply said, "Seven."

The next day, my husband was mute. He held up eight fingers, walked into the bedroom, and closed the door. I could hear him rummaging through the closet to find his old work clothes and tools.

"I think the kids have had enough good experience now," my husband said as he emerged from our bedroom in his bib overalls with a hammer in one hand and a saw in the other. "Renaldo is getting his own private sleeping quarters tonight."

"But Dad, Scamper and Renaldo will get lonely for each other. They've always lived together."

My husband faked hearing loss and proceeded to build the fastest segregated male rabbit hutch in history. But now we have one more problem. Our baby bunnies are growing up, and we hear they can become proud parents in a few months' time.

Is there anyone out there who can tell the difference between a male and a female bunny? If so, please call immediately.

Mother's Day Masquerade

Many people have asked me how I came up with the title for one of my books, Why Does My Mother's Day Potted Plant Always Die?

Well, I'm not exactly proud of this, but here goes.

On Mother's Day a while back, I was definitely ready to put in for early retirement. It had been one of those hectic Sundays with me trying to get all the kids ready for church on time.

My husband was off to a meeting somewhere. I had been around the house all morning squawking, "Why do you always lose your left shoe?" "We're going to be late!" "No, you may not wear your smelly tennis shoes." "We're going to be late!" "I want everyone to get in here and use the bathroom before we go—now!" "We're going to be late!" "Why do you always need a drink right when it's time to go?" "We're going to be late!"

Finally, I got all the kids into the car and raced down to the church. Once there, I quickly pushed all the kids down the aisle and plopped down on the bench totally frazzled, out of breath, and late.

Then we had one of those wonderful Mother's Day programs in which everyone on the program succeeded in making me feel terrible. I remember one particular gentleman who stood up and with much sincerity stated, "My mother never—no, never, not even one little time—raised her voice in our home."

I hung my head and glanced down at my tribe. I knew if they held an election for Mother of the Year, I would lose by ten votes, all cast by my own children.

After the flowing tributes were over, someone ordered all the mothers to stand up. Then they handed each stand-upper a beautiful little potted plant.

I took mine home and put it on the windowsill above my kitchen sink. I tried my best to keep it alive. First the leaves fell off. Then the stem started looking pale. I fertilized, watered, and chanted over it. I mean, letting your Mother's Day plant die must be a bad omen. But no matter what I did, it was lights out. My plant had definitely kicked the bucket.

Later, I went to my neighbor's house to borrow some eggs. When we went into her kitchen, I noticed this beautiful plant on her kitchen table with shiny leaves and vibrant stems bursting with enormous flowers. I commented on how beautiful the plant was.

"Oh, that old thing," my neighbor said. "It's just that puny potted plant they gave us in church on Mother's Day."

I felt like slowly melting and squeezing under the door in a quick exit. I knew I was the only mother on the planet who murdered all her Mother's Day potted plants. I was absolutely sure it was a barometer of my mothering abilities. I wasn't just depressed, I felt I needed to repent or something.

Luckily, nobody reported me to the authorities.

It's when all the pink carnation corsages are turning brown and wilting in the refrigerator that we mothers can heave a sigh of relief. If we can make it through Mother's Day without throwing in the towel, we're doing all right.

I'm finally learning not to worry about all those mothers I hear about on Mother's Day and don't measure up to. They don't exist. There are times when even the most serene mother feels that she qualifies for the Maternal Monster of the Year award.

All it really takes to survive as a mother is a good set of threats. These important verbal volleys are passed down from one generation to another much like cherished recipes and fine china from the old world.

Threats are great to use when you don't know how to get your kids to do something or quit doing something. One of the most commonly known methods is counting. This sort of threat originated when the first cavemom saw her cavechild scribbling on the cave walls with blunt rocks.

"Stop that!" the cavemom shouted.

Cavechild persisted.

"I'm going to count to three, and if you haven't put that rock down, I'm going to . . . one. . . two. . ."

At this point, Cavechild was grinning from ear to ear as he moved the rock closer and closer back toward the wall.

"Two and a half . . . two and three quarters . . . two and seven eighths." If it weren't for this kind of ancient threat, fractions would never have been invented.

"It" threats were next to appear on the historical time line. Ancient moms possessed limited vocabularies and had to rely on simple generic words.

"Knock *it* off! We'll have no more bone gnawing at the dinner table."

"Don't touch that mammoth pie! You don't know where *it's* been!"

"Don't you smile at me with your ape-like malocclusion. This is *it*!"

"All right, you little Homo sapien. I've had *it*!"

"You stop that groveling on all fours this instant or you'll really catch *it*."

When generic threats quit working, specific threats (with graphic descriptions of consequences to be faced) were invented. Mothers used this kind of threat to intimidate their children.

"Come down from there before you fall and break your neck."

"You'll shoot your eye out."

"Wash your hands or you'll get the worms."

"If you keep pulling ugly faces at your sister, one of these days your face will freeze like that."

After these scare tactics lost their pizzazz, our ancient predecessors resorted to the ultimate, perfected guilt-trip line handed own from every mother in one generation to another: "Well, I never gave my mother this much trouble."

After a snowstorm, I was standing in the doorway with my mom when I noticed my four-year-old shoveling snow into his mouth.

"Don't eat that," I yelled.

"Why?" he yelled back.

"Tell him it has little white worms in it," my mother whispered.

"Does it?"

"Does it what?"

"Does it have little white worms in it?"

"I don't know. What does that have to do with it? After my mother said that to me, I quit eating snow immediately," my mother answered.

So there you have it. Mother's Day comes but once a year, but maternal threats come in handy every day of the year and last forever.

RENEWAL PERIOD

While They Can Still Sniff 'Em

Most people wait until they die to spend much time in a cemetery. Even on Memorial Day, the visits are short, the remembering brief.

Many people are as uncomfortable with cemeteries as they are with life. But I believe cemeteries teach us more about living and more about ourselves than any place on earth, because cemeteries are constant reminders of what we are not.

Most of our living seems a frenzied attempt to define who we are with labels, titles, positions, and possessions. We come to define ourselves by what we have or what we do for a living. The actual living takes a backseat while we work for "security." But the only real constant about life is change.

Sooner or later we all realize there is no final destination where the bands are playing, the flags are waving, and we finally have all our dreams come true. The final destination constantly outdistances us. The joy of life is the journey.

In the end, we all finally discover we are not our house. (Having the biggest house on the block doesn't seem too important when we're eighty-seven and have to keep the place up.) We're not our car. (Getting from here to there is really the object.) We are not our spouse. (Some never marry. Husbands die. Wives leave.) We are not our children. (Children grow up, leave, and have their own families and lives.) We are not our occupation. (Someday we retire or get fired.) We are not our church job. (People actually survive without our blessings or cursings.) We are not even our name. (Names serve as simple identifiers that may change several times in our lives.)

That someone underneath all these layers is who we are. When we feel most alone, stripped down to our true selves, I think we will discover that it is our personal relationships with God, ourselves, our family, and our fellowmen that matter most.

It is largely with our families that we invest our dreams and hopes. It is with these precious few that we play out our lives.

There is no one else on this planet with whom we have more in common. Our families can't be replaced.

Who will care when we are gone? Who will hold us in their arms when we die? Who will miss our companionship, our quiet voice, the way we laugh, our gentle hands, our warm embrace? Who will care if we were here at all? Who we have loved and who have loved us—that will sum it all up.

Cemeteries remind us that life is precarious and that any day could be our last. Cemeteries equalize. Whether pope or peon, it doesn't take much space to put one under. Pretense, power, and possessions have no place here.

So on our remembering day, let's remember life is short—too short to leave ourselves unacquainted with who we really are, too short to leave the loving undone, the appreciation unfelt, the joy unembraced.

"I like to sniff her 'cause she smells so good," my dusty, besmudged four-year-old son says of his freshly bathed newborn sister.

So go ahead and decorate a few graves with flowers for the dead on Memorial Day. But more important, smell the flowers yourself—or better yet, give flowers to your living loved ones while they're still able to sniff 'em.

Halloween Hoots

I am definitely not one of those mothers who go all out for Halloween. You know the ones I mean. They sit on the front row in the gymnasium during the Halloween kindergarten assembly with a video camera taking pictures of Melvin in his homemade green satin stegosaurus costume complete with stuffed spikes and a six-foot-long tail.

When my five-year-old asked for help with his costume, I told him to put a raisin in his belly button and go as a cookie.

Halloween is simple when you have preschoolers. You

simply get them ready for bed in their usual pink or yellow blanket sleepers, paint a couple of whiskers under their nose with eyebrow pencil, and tell them they're bunnies. Then you drag them around enough blocks to get a big enough stash of candy to make you and your husband hyperactive for a week.

Actually, staying home to answer the door on Halloween is the most fun. You stay close to the front door for hours answering the doorbell for little children who sometimes have trouble taking in all this holiday business.

I remember last Halloween. The first time I answered the door and waited for the traditional "trick or treat," I was greeted with total silence. The eye holes in the fuzzy-orange-wigged clown mask didn't match up with the eyes of the four-year-old occupant.

"Say, 'Trick or treat,'" I heard some dark adult figure growl from the sidewalk.

Still silence.

"Jason, say 'Trick or treat,' for Pete's sake!"

Jason was now sucking on a purple and green sucker and had it stuck halfway into the eye hole of his face mask.

Suddenly I saw Jason being jerked back down the sidewalk.

The next time I answered the door, all six trick-or-treaters were complaining because their "dorky" mom had made them wear their coats and nobody could see their costumes.

My elderly neighbor knows how to celebrate this holiday. She always dresses up in elaborate costumes to scare my kids when they come to her door. Of course, she knows they won't be scared, and they know they won't be scared, but she gives out great treats. She always makes them come inside to warm up and sing her a song before she hands over the goodies. I guess when you get old, you've been a child, had children, and had the children go. So you find ways to bring the children back.

My children are getting too old for Halloween to be fun anymore. They count their Snickers candy bars before they go to sleep, so as to keep me from swiping them while they're dead to the world. Now my oldest children have even resorted to hiding their entire candy stash from me. It takes nearly all night to find their bags.

My husband and I like to buy the Halloween candy early and make sure it's something we especially like. For some reason it always disappears before the big day, and we have to go out and buy more.

Don't let anybody tell you Halloween is for kids.

Thanksgiving Treasure

Most of my Thanksgiving Day memories are steaming with oven-roasted turkey or fresh yeast rolls. There are always crowds of people wandering through those memories too... uncles with whiskers and bad breath who want to kiss you ... brothers and sisters who cap their teeth with black olives and blow bubbles in their fruit punch. The grown-ups are always murmuring in the dining room, stopping only long enough to say, "All right, you kids, settle down out there!"

But one year there were no turkeys, no relatives, no black olives, and no fruit punch. My husband and I had plans to go to Grandma's for the usual feast, but a busy nightlong vigil made for a quick change of plans.

On the night before Thanksgiving Day, each of our children had taken a turn becoming ill with the stomach flu. My husband and I ran from bed to bed. We had the washing machine going all night.

Just when it appeared we had seen the worst of it and the children were starting to go back to sleep, it hit my husband and me. By morning the whole family looked like death warmed over.

That Thanksgiving the children were too weak to play or wiggle or even fight. There were no visitors. Nobody wanted to catch what we had. There was no feast. No one could keep anything down even if anyone could get up and fix it.

It was a quiet day. There was no TV blaring in the corner of the room or radio broadcasting from the bookshelf. The rocking chair creaked slowly next to the piano in the living room while my husband took turns rocking the children to sleep.

As I sat on our worn sofa stroking a child's small head in my lap and cradling another in the bend of my arm, I did a lot of thinking—thinking about what I was grateful for. I wasn't distracted by football games, turkey, or relatives.

As I rubbed my child's sweaty forehead and looked into his eyes, it occurred to me that it wasn't the neighborhood I lived n, or the new carpet or lack of it, that really mattered. Everything that really mattered was who I loved and who loved me.

The whole richness of life was contained in the embryotic relationships that were growing, developing, and changing within the walls of my own home. My deep and meaningful relationships with people, not my possessions or positions, would ultimately become the final tally of my life.

I realized that most of the problems our family faced came from being overcommitted, from having too much to do. Our relationships suffered when we couldn't bring ourselves to say no to other people, to properly unorder our lives so there was enough time to take walks together, play board games on the kitchen table, tell jokes while we scrubbed the pots and pans, or snuggle in the rocking chair as we watched the stars appear in the night sky.

It really isn't quality time but lots of unscheduled quantity time that matters. We spend the most time with what we truly love.

We didn't dress or eat or even talk much that day. My thoughts were slow, unhurried, and singular. I looked at my husband and my children differently that day, as if I were seeing them for the first time. I noticed the unusual upward turn of my husband's brow, the circular mixture of blue, green, and brown in my daughter's eyes, the soft, satin feel of my baby's cheeks.

My family was all that seemed real that day. The rest of the world seemed out of focus, somewhere out there in the distance. Everything that really mattered was rocking quietly next to the piano or snuggled deep in my arms. I was intensely aware of the swelling emotion I felt for each child and for my husband. I loved them more than I could express.

That evening, we all sat around the kitchen table and took turns telling each other what we were grateful for. Later, we bowed our heads as our three-year-old led us in prayer.

"Heavenly Father, thank thee for all the guys and Mom and Dad. Amen."

Our feast that evening consisted of one banana Popsicle per person. I've never had a day or a banana Popsicle that tasted so good.

Christmas with Children

Somewhere back in the far recesses of my mind I can remember a Christmas without children. My husband and I had been married for a grand total of five months. We were expecting our first child, but the patter of little feet had not yet invaded our peaceful existence.

I remember actually sleeping in on Christmas morning. I remember having in the front room a Christmas tree no one had pulled over and ornaments no one had tugged off, sucked on, licked, or squished up.

I remember actually being alone in the house and peacefully listening to Christmas carols on the stereo. Our carpet was not decorated with juice stains, and our sliding glass door was not adorned with dozens of fingerprints.

Wrapping paper was not flying through the air or working its way through a baby's digestive system when my new husband and I opened our presents that quiet morning.

Later, when we walked into the kitchen for breakfast, the cabinets were not locked or even tied together. We ate a leisurely breakfast that no one in the entire family threw onto the floor, flipped across the table with a fork, or oozed out between their teeth in a spray.

During the day, we did unheard of, spontaneous things like running outside and playing in the snow together without first finding, grunting, and tugging up a dozen boots and gloves. We didn't have to zip and snap a half dozen coats or position as many hats and scarves. We didn't even have to undo all this bundling work thirty seconds later after too many little bodies stepped out into the cold and suddenly realized they had to go to the bathroom.

We visited family and friends without having to take along a suitcase of supplies. We drove in a small sedan with no one fistfighting in the backseat.

When we read the story of the famous family in Luke, there was no one to argue over who got to be Mary and no one running to the bathroom to get a toilet plunger for a staff and a towel for a turban so he could be Joseph. There was no one taping a cotton ball to underpants so he or she could be the lamb, and no baby to tumble out of the manger, banging his head on he floor.

There were no stockings lined up in a row, no giggling, ripping, taping, and frantic wrapping of tin can pencil holders for Mom and Dad behind locked doors. No one begged me to read "The Night Before Christmas" or to sing a duet when I played "Jingle Bells" or "Silent Night" on the piano.

There were no grade school Christmas programs to make costumes for, no junior high chorus concerts to attend, no piano recitals, and no Santas to visit at Cub Scout pack night.

I don't know how we stood it. Talk about boring! Thank heaven for the chaotic, child-filled Christmases we savor now.

Christmas with children has its own special magic.

Every year I promise my children that if they sleep in until four o'clock on Christmas morning, I will not slop around the house all morning looking for my sense of humor and let my head fall into the cinnamon rolls at breakfast. It's a good thing events never work out according to contract at my house.

At some unholy hour, approximately twenty-three minutes and seventeen seconds after my husband and I have retired for the night, ten shadows appear at the foot of our bed. The first thing I hear is heavy, labored breathing, then. . .

"Do you think they're awake?"

"Somebody check the clock."

'Anybody got a flashlight?"

"Yeah, I do."

"Well, shine it on 'em and see if their eyes are shut."

Then a cold, wet nose touches mine as a small, sticky finger pries my eyelid open and someone yells, "Hey, Mom! You awake?"

"No," I mumble and roll over.

At this precise moment, ten shadows pounce on two lethargic lumps in the master bed.

"Oh, kids, go back to bed. It's too early," my husband groans while some child is ricocheting off his chest and another is beaming Morse code flashlight signals up his nose.

"Dad! Dad! Dad! It's Christmas."

"It's not Christmas. You silly kids have your days mixed up. Go back to bed."

"But we can't go back to sleep now."

"We're too excited."

My husband and I like to extend this moment. It's our last chance to be in charge all day. Once we leave our bedroom, all parental control flies out of the window and gives way to the children's hour. The pandemonium that is Christmas begins.

First the family room becomes bewitched with the lighting of the tree. Then there is the frantic ripping of paper and the lowering of bulging stockings. Then there is the slurping of wet tongues on peppermint and the fresh scent of oranges losing their skins. It's loud, confusing, messy, and wonderful.

RENEWAL PERIOD

If there's anything even more fun than watching your young children enjoy Christmas, it's watching your big kids watch your little kids enjoy Christmas. Then comes game playing, toy trading, turkey eating, welcoming friends and relatives, and cleaning up in the kitchen.

Later in the afternoon, as the children lounge drowsily on the sofa and the house is quiet, a sad thought comes. Night is coming and soon Christmas will be gone for yet another year.

On December the twenty-sixth, we find there is nothing so over as Christmas.

CHAPTER 4
FAMILY HISTORY
INDUSTRIAL ERA
MEDIOCRE PERIOD

My two-year-old just ate some ants
Before he tipped over four houseplants.
My mate says, "Hon, how 'bout a date?"
I'm sorry dear, I'm running late.
Bishop says, "We need more work,"
But I'm already half berserk.
My doctor says to exercise,
But I like fat upon my thighs.
Can't get my visiting teaching done,
My car's a wreck and so's my son.
Sometimes I wonder what I'll do —
That's when I always get the flu.

Telephone Etiquette

Children should not be allowed within ten feet of the telephone if parents desire to retain any semblance of pride, privacy, or purchasing power.

I remember my early days of motherhood when I really tried to teach my children the proper way to answer the telephone. We rehearsed over and over again the opening phrase I wanted them to use: "Hello. May I help you?"

When my children had the phrase memorized, I lectured them on ways to avoid answering questions from strangers and told them not to volunteer any information.

One day when I was busy in the bathroom and couldn't get to the telephone, I heard my three-year-old answer it. I listened attentively, waiting to hear the fruits of my telephone lessons.

"Helwo," she said. "Who's dis? What you want?" (Opening phrase down the tube.)

She paused. "Are you a stranger?" she continued. (Rule number two down the tube.) There was a long pause again.

When she felt assured the caller was no longer a stranger, she broke rule number three and volunteered unnecessary information. "No, Mommy can't come to da phone. She's in the bathroom." (Then she told the caller *exactly* what I was doing in the bathroom.)

Children also like to keep their parents hopping when it comes time for Mom and Dad to answer the telephone. While my children are supposed to be sleeping, I have a sneaking suspicion they crawl out of bed, lower themselves out of the window with their crib sheets, and attend "how to annoy your parents when they're on the telephone" school. Why else would my children strictly adhere to the same age-correlated rules whenever the telephone rings and it happens to be for me?

As soon as I try to have an adult conversation on the telephone, all children between the age of birth and two years immediately start crying. Children between the ages of two and four immediately have to go to the bathroom and need help.

This telephone malady also affects all male children between the ages of four and eight. They immediately run next to me talking on the phone then wrap something firmly around their necks, and try to hang themselves. Female children in this age group try to use the mom's phone conversations as the perfect time to start an argument.

Children between the ages of eight and twelve always think of some absolutely nonsensical question that must be answered by their parent in the next microsecond or they will keel over and die. The best way to ask this question is to silently creep over to Mom from behind and shove your face so close to hers that it makes her go cross-eyed. Then repeat sixty-seven times, "Mom, Mom, Mom . . ."

When Mom finally answers and says, "Son, I'm on the phone. I'll talk to you later," Son immediately changes tactics and starts poking her on the arm or pushing his nose against hers, wailing, "But, Mom, I have to ask you something."

At this point, most parents are making silent death-threat faces and wildly gesturing at their obnoxious children to scare them off as they try to keep their voice calm and sedate while finishing their telephone conversation.

Contrary to popular belief, children in the teenage years solve many parental telephone problems. They stay on the phone so long that no one else can get through, so Mom and Dad can rest easy, never knowing what life-altering calls they've missed.

When the kids leave home, they all learn the meaning of the word collect and how it pertains to telephone charges. Parents find a whole new meaning for the phrase phone bill, as it inches toward and then over the price of their home mortgage.

When Alexander Graham Bell said, "Mr. Watson, come here. I want you!" it was probably because he needed someone to tend Alexander, Junior, while he finished inventing the telephone.

Bread-Baking Ballads

I have a confession to make. In a day when everyone seems to be happy with store-bought bread (which has enough air in it to float out of the plastic bag and into the toaster), I love to bake bread, even if I only get around to it every other year. After all, bread making has kept my marriage together.

First there's that wonderful therapeutic exercise of kneading the dough. I make the best bread when I'm mad at my husband. All those unvented emotions are unleashed upon the unsuspecting dough, and my adrenaline is put to good use. A good punching session with the dough is more productive than one with my husband, because the dough is less likely to punch back.

Maybe the thing I like best about this whole affair is the chance to lick the dough off my fingers when the kids aren't looking. My mother's not around to tell me my stomach will swell up like a balloon from eating raw dough and that I'll float away in pain. Now I'm the mother and I get to scare the kids to death.

Then there's the aroma of the baking bread that comes circling up through the heat vents into every room of the house, and the warm cozy way the kitchen feels when the heat and baking smells are escaping from the oven.

Maybe I could have resisted this addiction if the loaves of bread didn't look quite so appetizing as they lay on their sides cooling in straight rows on the white cotton dish towel. Maybe I could have resisted if the sweet butter glaze didn't melt so smoothly over the spiraling curves of hot cinnamon rolls that are bulging with plump raisins, and smelling of cinnamon and sugar.

Maybe I should break the habit and just pick up a couple of loaves at the store. But after mixing, kneading, shaping, and the anticipation of waiting for the dough to rise, I guess anything would taste pretty good.

Homemade bread, still steaming from the oven, spread with creamy butter and golden, dripping honey, will wear down my defenses every time.

I have only one word of advice for those of you who might still be living as a store-bought-disadvantaged person. Don't try baking bread yourself. If you try baking bread, even once, you may get hooked for life.

But what a way to go.

Interior Decorating with Class

Parenthood has a rather surprising way of determining your interior decorating tastes. My husband and I recently picked out new carpet for the family room. We discovered we've changed from two people with fair-to-middling decorating taste into a couple who ask only one question for every household purchase: "Will this color hide poop and barf stains?"

The distressed look in furniture is popular now, but we don't have to shell out big bucks for that look. Our kids made an instant distressed look dining room table when they used it as a barricade during their latest fight. They volleyed every saber-toothed, deadly six-ton object within reach at each other while my husband and I were out on a date. When we arrived home, we found the children's skulls were unscratched (the mental capacity of the brains inside those skulls is another matter). But the table didn't fare so well.

Having children also tends to change parental definitions of many common household objects. Take doors, for instance. My children honestly believe doors are mechanical parts of the house used for making potholes in the drywall directly opposite the doorknob. They are also dead sure furniture makers leave a space between the bed mattress and the floor for the purpose of stuffing away two weeks' worth of dirty underwear, banana peelings, candy wrappers, loose change, unfinished homework, used bandages, and tissue.

I ask you, why do these small people who populate my home believe heat vents are like the all-day-and-night tellers the banks use? My kids make daily deposits of meltable wax crayons, Legos, and a varied assortment of moldy kiddy cuisine in the masked or crumbled state. When they tire of this activity, they use heat vents for walkie-talkies through which they yell at each other from bedroom to bedroom.

While I'm trying to peacefully rock the baby to sleep, I hear strange voices rising from the heat vents, screaming, "Hey, Jordan! Can you hear me?"

"Yeah, I hear you."

"Your mother wears army boots!"

I'd also like to know why all children seem to think the flush handles on the back of toilets are for decoration only? Why do they think bathroom mirrors are reflective easels, great for making utterly tasteless toothpaste murals? My children also use bathroom mirrors to watch themselves turning their eyelids and lips inside out, practicing to impress their girlfriends at school.

Hampers definitely aren't for dirty clothes. Dirty clothes are tossed about the floor in a well-organized typhoon fashion.

Hampers are for the fresh, clean clothes Mom placed on the end of the bed and was naive enough to believe would be put away in the chest of drawers.

Interior decorating with kids is easy. I have no trouble in choosing between the sleek, modern look and cozy country charm. I go for a menagerie of early-relative furnishings and the very popular lived-in look every time.

Hold On to Your Insanity

If you decide to produce more than the national average of 1.4 children during your married life, a pressing dilemma will eventually have to be faced. It is not an easy issue and it takes fortitude to face it squarely: What does one do with a .4 child? Somewhere after about child 4.7 or 5.3, you'll eventually find yourself standing in line for hours to use the bathroom, and a really stupid thought will race through your mind: I wonder if we ought to get a bigger house or add on to our present quarters.

This is a dangerous thought. If you buy or build a bigger house, you will probably not live to see the day your mortgage is paid off. If you decide to add on, it's like making a detailed blueprint of instructions telling how to drive you and your spouse stark-raving crazy, one slow, painful step at a time.

Most people who decide to add on to their house do so because they have too many children for too little house. Having too many children also has a tendency to compound the problem of too little money. This is the category my husband and I fell into. So we decided to do most of the work ourselves. Now, this may sound like a good money-saving idea, but if you think things went well for us, just think again.

The first time I saw my husband take an ax to our front porch, I panicked. "What on earth are you doing!"

"Calm down, Jan. I'm just starting to work on the addition," Ross answered.

"But you're—"

"I know. We'll just have to live without using the front door for a while. No big deal. Relax."

Crash! Crunch! Kabam! Suddenly my husband was hauling away our entire front porch. If one of our children forgot and raced out of the front door as usual, he ended up spread-eagled at the bottom of a ten-foot pit.

When you add on to houses, you generally eliminate old entrances and create new ones. The entire left side of my house was demolished and exposed to the elements. A cotton sheet separated me from the best Mother Nature had to offer—hail, sleet, rain, wind, and tons of dirt—for weeks.

Just when my husband and a ragtag group of construction workers down on their luck got into the thick of things, all my kids came down with chicken pox. It is not a summer I like to recall. What do you do when your front entrance is demolished, the entire left side of your house is no more, and all your kids are sick? You start digging another humongous hole for your children to fall into, that's what.

My husband measured and soon dug a black pit big enough to bury the entire family and all the neighbor kids. Not being one to avoid a little dirt, I decided to jump down into the muddy hole with him and get to work with my own shovel and pick. I held ropes for chalk lines, threw rocks into piles, and often wondered what on earth we were trying to do.

My husband, of course, was in heaven. He loved the work. He spent long hours at the office and then worked grueling hours in the pit until dark, digging, hammering, and measuring. He was chasing the long-sought, impossible dream of creating a private bathroom for himself where he could hide out when the going gets tough right before dinner. He was a driven man.

When the summer was over and the last grass seed had been planted around our new, beautiful, finished addition, Ross and I ceremoniously marched into our new private bathroom with fine-stemmed glasses and some grape juice. With the children pounding on the locked door yelling, "I'm hungry! Jordan hit me! What are you guys doing in there?" we clicked our glasses together, took a long, slow sip, and smiled.

Deseret Industry Treasure Hunts

If you haven't shopped at Deseret Industries, you're missing out on some terrific discoveries. Thrift store shopping is not for wimps, but it does require one to possess an amateur archaeologist's naivete. You have to be willing to put in long, grueling hours to uncover your treasures. But when you make that important find, all the dirty work doesn't matter. You're intoxicated. Given any spare time, you're ready to dig in and make the next important discovery.

My mother always told me there's a rule decreed in heaven, or somewhere else equally indisputable, which states: "If you regularly donate to Deseret Industries when you have extra, you'll be able to find what you need there when times get tight."

I am living proof of her prophecy. I regularly sack up anything we're not using and take it to the loading dock in the rear of D.I. When times have gotten a little tight, I will invariably find that much-needed coat for Jordan, dress for Arianne, or toy truck just in time for Jacob's birthday.

When I was a young girl, my family often spent time shopping at Deseret Industries. I was one of eight daughters, and we had to learn to make over and make do with what we could find there. I remember looking timidly around me, embarrassed to see anyone I knew.

My attitude quickly changed when my friends at school accused me of being spoiled because I had so many cute clothes. When I had to babysit, pick cherries, or knit hotpads for my school clothes money, Deseret Industries was a real lifesaver.

I've recently discovered another kind of treasure at my favorite thrift store. It was while shoveling through mounds of coats that I uncovered Monica. Monica is an attractive mother about my age. I found her at my elbow, rummaging through coats for her children also. We began talking, and soon I knew all the ages, gender, and sizes of her six children—and she knew all mine.

"Oh, look." Monica smiled proudly, holding up a nice purple coat. "This one would be perfect for your six-year-old girl. Does she like purple?"

"Purple and pink are her favorite colors," I answered. "How about this one for your ten-year-old boy? It's not even worn on the cuffs or under the arms."

"He doesn't like zippers," she answered. "Let me know if you find one with snaps."

We searched, hunted, and inspected coats for ourselves and each other until our arms ached. After about an hour, we each lined up our selections in one long line on an empty table and gave each other our final evaluations.

"I don't think your eight-year-old boy will wear that one," Monica commented. "It looks too much like a girl's coat."

"You're right," I said, putting it back on the rack. "What do you think of this one?"

"That's a nice one. He'll wear that one," she answered.

"If I were you, I'd take the blue one over the green one. It'll hide the dirt better," I said, pointing to a coat in her lineup. "That's for the one that likes to play football, right?"

"You're right," Monica answered. "I'm glad you thought of that."

By the time Monica and I left that day, we each had our arms full of great little coats at great little prices.

Monica is not the only treasure I've discovered at my favorite store, but she's by far one of the best.

A Year's Supply of Mice Is Nice

It's a good idea to secure a year's supply of food and, where possible, fuel to last a year. This is very sound advice, especially if you like the sound of mice. It's difficult to pack in food without welcoming a few uninvited guests.

When I was growing up, it was a well-known fact that Mr. Mouse lived in our storage room. No one but me seemed unduly alarmed over his presence. Every time I was asked to retrieve a bottle or two of peaches for dinner dessert, my heart started racing.

I figured Mr. Mouse deserved to endure a heart attack along with me, so I always announced my presence before I opened the door to the dark, mysterious room. I walked sheepishly up to the closed storage room door, then suddenly beat on the door with both fists.

Next I lowered my voice and recounted my intentions. "Mr. Mouse," I said, loud enough to be heard through the door, "I, Horrible Human, am about to enter this room. If you happen to be out in the open or plan to run up someone's legs, forget it. I have with me the ultimate mouse mangler machine, and I would like nothing better than for some stupid mouse to show his face so I can dispose of his rotten little body once and for all."

Next I tucked my pant legs into my socks just in case anybody got any ideas. Then I'd creak open the door and thump a few more times as I sidestepped into the room with my eyes half shut. The next move was a beeline for the first Kerr bottle in reach and a mad dash back to the door, slamming it shut behind me.

Now that I'm a mature middle-aged mother with my own storage room, I no longer act so immature. Now I make my kids go in there, just like my sainted mother before me.

As all food storage experts know, the first evidences of several friendly, unwanted lodgers in the lima beans are the telltale little black doo-doo on the shelves. At first this is not alarming, and you simply try to convince yourself that your dust particles are growing.

Eventually these telltale signs can no longer be ignored. The call to action is most likely made at midnight just as your good soldier is about to drop off to sleep.

"I heard scratching!" you scream as you rocket straight out of the sheets and kick your husband in the ribs. "There's a mouse in the storage room! You've got to go in there and get him."

Now, don't ask me why husbands are always instantly enlisted to be the mouse hunters. It's the same reason why wives are always the ones to remove and replace the empty cardboard roll on the toilet paper spindle.

Mouse hunting is not a quiet enterprise, even when you find the entire nest in your spaghetti-ends box. The last time I volunteered my husband to march in the mouse-enemy army, I heard the soft padding of feet up the steps and out the back door. I was sitting in bed clutching the sheets around my neck when I heard the loudest, most horrendous thundering. It sounded like garbage cans being smashed into smithereens with baseball bats.

In time, Ross crawled back into bed without saying a word. "Well?" I asked, still sitting straight up in bed. "What happened?"

"I don't want to talk about it," Ross answered.

"Did you get them? I can't go to sleep until I know."

"Yeah, I got them. There was a whole family with babies and everything. I don't feel so great about it, so go to sleep, will ya?"

"Babies? Gee, I didn't know mice had babies. I'm sorry I made you do it, really I am."

"Yeah, well, it's all right, I guess," Ross answered. "It's either them or us, I guess."

"I guess."

"I don't even mind them getting our whole case of spaghetti-ends," Ross finished. "They were kinda cute."

Storing food is still a sound idea, but sometimes it's not as easy as it may seem.

A Mother's Basic Guide to Creative Suffering

Mothers are generally very good at suffering. The only problem is that no one seems to notice, and all this suffering is in vain. That's why I'm in the process of developing a new course titled, "A Mother's Basic Guide to the Proper Techniques of Creative Suffering." Properly practiced, motherly suffering is an art—a complex network of subtle and highly sophisticated techniques. It takes a little work, but every mother can become a noticeable and proficient sufferer if she desires.

As part of my course, I'll be selling tapes similar to those foreign language tapes where the instructor says a phrase and then pauses while the student repeats back the gibberish. Mothers will be required to memorize and pass off these phrases that are guilt-inducing for their ungrateful offspring.

Phrase 1: "Go ahead and enjoy yourself. I don't mind staying home alone."

Phrase 2: "Hello, (insert your child's name here). This is your mother. Remember me?"

Phrase 3: (Look pathetic. Wait for someone to say, "What's the matter?" Then repeat:) "Oh, it's nothing, nothing at all. The doctor says I still have a little time left."

Phrase 4: "When you're grown, I hope you have triplets just like you."

Phrase 5: "Why are you yelling? I'm only trying to make you happy."

Phrase 6: "Who do I cook for, clean for? Who did I walk the floor with every night for six months?"

Because most children are sensitive to the fact that their births probably in some way physically impaired their mother, I'll teach mothers to use this guilt for constructive purposes by attributing all maternal ailments to the birth of their children. Such as: bad back—caused by the birth of Becky; gray hair—Rufus; postnasal drip—Dorcas; brittle bones—Brian; menopause—the twins; poochy paunch—Phyllis; and the tendency to occasionally act weird —Wilford.

You see, the agonizing process of birth entitles all mothers to lifelong homage from their children. Mothers should continually remind their forgetful children of this great debt. Children should be constantly reminded that never, during their entire lifetime, will they know as much as their mother.

Another technique I'll help mothers master will be to always get up at 5:30 a.m. no matter what time it really is. The image of martyrdom is one of the most essential of all the tools of creative maternal suffering. True, lasting guilt cannot be induced without it. For instance: When fixing the family toast, always take the burnt heel, and make sure your children notice that you took it.

Children should be constantly reminded of all the things you are denying yourself on their account. When you have to miss something important to watch Tim play his part as a talking rock in his third grade assembly, make sure he knows that the last thing you want him to know is that you missed something important. If you're not missing anything important, make something up.

When your children argue about doing small chores, proceed to sigh your best Joan of Arc groan, then proceed to do the job yourself, in front of them—in slow motion. When all else fails to get the kids to jump, mothers everywhere can rely on the phrase that won the honorary annual Maternal Martyr award in 1956, namely, "You'll be sorry . . . when I'm dead."

So, mothers everywhere, don't despair. You, too, with practice, can conquer the difficult techniques of creative suffering.

Harvest of Havoc

A while back I read one of those lovely, homespun magazine articles about parenting. It gave me a guilt complex I try to get rid of every spring during planting season.

In this article, the parents happily involved their children in all gardening and yard work tasks.

"After all," the wise parent was quoted as saying, "we are raising more than carrots."

So I've tried. Honestly, I've tried, but gardening and kids have yet to raise more than heck at my home. I, too, am raising more than carrots—I'm raising terrorists.

Grandparents, kindhearted but terribly forgetful, often tell mothers of young children, "Oh, my dear, as soon as you blink, they'll all be grown up."

Don't believe them, and for heaven's sake, don't ever try it—blinking, I mean. As soon as you do, your child is likely to terrorize the neighborhood.

My young son tried to help our elderly neighbor water his garden one spring afternoon. He toddled over to Mr. Retired's showplace garden on his cute little chubby legs, found a can with a spigot, and proceeded to do his good deed for the day. The problem was, the can with the spigot didn't turn out to be a watering can. In two minutes flat, this son had dumped an entire gallon of gasoline on our neighbors' pride and joy.

The next day, while I was planting petunias in the front yard flower bed, my three- and four-year-old daughters ran toward me yelling, "Mom! Look what we found floating down the ditch."

They each held a beautiful, perfectly formed purple petunia, root and all, in their palms.

"That's strange," I said, taking the flowers. "I hate to see these pretty flowers go to waste. I guess I'll just plant them here with the pink ones I'm already planting. Purple and pink go nicely together."

For ten minutes, these daughters ran back and forth from the ditch and proudly presented me with about thirty of the mysterious purple petunias. That's when I noticed my two-year-old son over at the flower bed owned by Mr. Retired (yes, the same one with the dead garden). My young son was pulling my neighbor's petunias out as fast as he could, then racing over to the ditch and tossing them in. Whereupon his sisters, about a block down, would "discover" them floating in the ditch and bring them back to me. I had now successfully replanted my neighbor's entire flower bed in my yard.

My neighbors moved soon after that. I never could figure out why they gave up their yard for trailer court asphalt.

CHAPTER 5

FAMILY HISTORY

THE AGE OF EXPLORATION
SPACED-OUT PERIOD

I have no dates, my dress is old.
The cheese at lunch is growing mold.
I failed the test, was late for math.
Miss Slim in gym says, "Take a bath!"
I have a tin grin in my mouth.
My father says we're moving south.
Grow up, slow down, you're late, they say—
I think I'll pack and move away.
What's that? I do not have to stay?
. . . I think I'll wait till Saturday.

Terminal Teenage-itis

Other mothers have been warning me for years about becoming a mother of teenagers. But I wasn't ready to listen to their harder-times-ahead stories when I was in the middle of five preschoolers down with chicken pox, or when I was toilet training tots, suffering postpartum blues, or nine and a half months pregnant.

I didn't really believe their scare tactics. I mean, how could a child who would use the bathroom unassisted be all bad? How could a child who didn't require hand feeding every two hours be someone to complain about? I didn't appreciate their comments, and besides, I didn't intend to have teenagers. I knew all my children would accidentally kill themselves by leaping off the top of the refrigerator before they reached age two anyway.

Mothers of teens were always telling me about the "monster school" up in the east part of town.

"I sent that school my sweet grade-school child," these mothers insisted, "and they sent me back a monster."

These mothers were referring to the local junior high school. I just knew they were exaggerating. I mean, my oldest child was in fifth grade and she hadn't started growing any fangs yet.

But time passed.

Then something happened. My daughter walked in the door and I greeted her with my usual, "Well, how was school today, dear?"

She scowled at me and replied, "Why do you want to know?"

I was getting suspicious.

A week or two later I asked her if she wanted to go shopping with me.

She looked me over from head to toe and replied, "Not if you're going to go dressed like that."

In the past, I had to drag her in the bathroom for baths. Lately, she's staying so long in the bathroom that her younger brothers and sisters think she's just one of the fixtures and try to throw their dirty clothes on her.

She locks herself in her bedroom for hours and turns up the radio so loud that all insects and rodents have gladly packed their bags and given up residence.

When I asked her to help me with the dishes, she shouted, "I hate this family! You don't understand me. Why don't you just get off my back?"

If my suspicions are correct, I have been initiated. This mother-of-teens club isn't as much fun as I thought it would be.

There is a new person in my home, and I'm inflicted with terminal flashback-itis. Every time my daughter struts proudly around the house in the latest hairstyle and fashion statement, I can't help but remember how she looked in her diapers as she waddled down the hall toward her crib.

When she screams, "I hate you," I can't help remembering when she used to gently pat my cheeks, rub her pug nose against mine, and say, "I love you, Mommy, bigger than a brontosaurus."

When she gets embarrassed to show me to the neighbors because I wear those geeky polyester pants and orthopedic shoes, I remember the time she danced around in the yard in front of the neighbors without wearing anything at all.

No one ever told me becoming a mother to teens meant mourning. No one ever told me I'd have to say good-bye to a twelve-year-old I knew and get acquainted with a thirteen-year-old stranger. It's not as much that I dislike the job, it's just that I'm having a hard time letting go of the child I knew.

She used to pull her little sister aside and say, "Hey, you want to play teenagers?" I thought they were so cute, experimenting with my makeup, wearing my clothes, and high-heeled shoes. Now my teenage daughters no longer smear the lipstick from their mouth to their nose, and they wouldn't be caught dead in anything I wear.

She used to wear a perpetual smile. Now she can go from angry to sad, happy, silly, and disgusting in seventeen seconds.

When she stands next to me now I can't reach down and pat her on top of the head, because her head is higher than my own. Maybe that's what it's all about, for then come the moments when I can almost remember what it was like when I was her age. I start tripping over my parental pedestal when I recall what it was like handling rejection from boys, getting a report card every time I turned around, making the team, wearing the right thing, having the right figure (or, heaven help you, any figure at all), taking tests, making or unmaking friends, having zits, wrestling with oily hair, and knowing without a doubt that I had the biggest fanny since Harry Hippo.

My teenage daughter isn't tagging behind me now, trying to keep up. In truth, I'm tagging behind her. Maybe sometime, if I'm lucky, she'll turn and wait up for me awhile at the crossroad from childhood to maturity—just long enough for me to wish her well as she chooses her own precarious road to travel.

Homemade Humiliation

Most professionals have at least one immensely momentous moment in which they desperately need to look good. Progress up the work world ladder depends on a certain boardroom presentation, a special interview on camera, a dinner date with the boss, or a perfectly worded recommendation.

Whatever the self-promoting event, it's abundantly clear that the rest of your professional life depends on your ability to pull off "the biggie" without a hitch. At such crucial events it is necessary to not wear your spare glasses (repaired with a Tinkerbell bandage), or drool on your tie, or sneeze into the microphone.

Such a perspiration presentation came for my husband the other day. Right at the climax of his momentous speech, he raised his fist to emphasize the crucial point. He noticed that everyone was staring at his wrist instead of oooing and ahhhing at his great intelligence. When he turned his arm to see what everyone was glaring at, he noticed our baby daughter's crocheted little pink bootie dangling from the wrist of his long-sleeved, freshly starched shirt.

Ah, the joys of parenting.

As every parent knows, even the best-laid plans for the perfect corporate image regularly turn into Gerber mush when you happen to have kids. But at least my husband can pretend he's smart for eight hours and impress the bigwigs with only an occasional goof while he's at the office. Things normally go pretty well unless my husband is naive enough to bring someone home to meet the family.

The last time my husband brought his boss home for lunch (notice, I say "last" because he never dared come again) I took great pains to make sure everything was just right. While we were dining, our young son slipped under the table unnoticed and proceeded to paint elaborate designs on the boss's grey wool slacks with a red marker.

I, on the other hand, happen to play office right here at home. Every time I get an important editor on the line, some kid will pick up the other telephone and make pig snorts into the receiver.

At a recent author's reception, I was making my acceptance speech when all eyes turned from me to the refreshment table, where my young son was stuffing layered sandwiches, eclairs, and salted nuts into his suit coat pocket while slurping up the Hawaiian Delight straight from the punch bowl with his straw.

I have no more pride. All my greatest fears of public humiliation have happened. Children have a way of keeping their parents' careers in check, their pretense in perspective, and their egos with egg on them.

Without kids, I have a feeling, we'd all actually start believing we were pretty hot stuff. But with children, we see ourselves as we really are—vulnerable adults playing hard at being grown-ups, all the while protecting that little child, that lost child, who once was and still is ourselves.

It Hurts When They Go Away

I have a sneaking suspicion that if they held a parental election to pass a worldwide year-around school program, it would pass by a landslide. A few of the more enlightened schools are in session during the times that try a mother's soul, but too many of us are still left with homebound, bored, and batty children all summer long.

Summer vacation never starts out this way, of course. I always start the summer doing exciting things like giving my children karate lessons. Later I regret my stupidity and tell the children not to bother me with their sibling self-defense fighting unless there's definite unconsciousness.

I always start the summer with ideas for intellectually stimulating museum excursions, numerous library visits, and exciting mother-taught cooking classes. Later I find myself saying, "I don't care if you've seen that movie six times. Go in there and watch television."

I start the summer dutifully giving the children piano lessons. As the months stretch on, I find myself sitting directly in front of a fan on high power, stuffing my ears with plugs, my mouth with aspirin, and my mind with a strong desire to develop early deafness.

I love summer at home with all the kids all day, really I do. Well, mostly I do. Well, sometimes I do. Summer teaches me to greatly admire my children's classroom teachers, who always seem amazingly stable and sane.

A while back, I went to the doctor to have my warts burned off. Those darn warts of mine had been hanging around for such a long time annoying me, I wanted to get rid of them.

The doctor was very polite as he proceeded to burn my warty flesh to smithereens. It was such a relief to think I might finally be rid of them. When the shock wore off and the pain hit, I wondered why on earth I'd been so anxious.

Funny, but those old warts were part of me. They may have been bothersome, but they were mine. I'm going to miss that familiar bump on my left heel that made walking in shoes a real pain, that obnoxious growth on my right finger that made typing feel as if I was pricking myself with a pin over and over, those numerous twitches on my right knee that reminded me whenever I knelt that I was Warty Wilma.

I'm like that on the first day of school.

At first it seems like a relief to get my little annoyances neatly packed off for six hours a day. Then the pain hits, and I wonder why I was ever so anxious.

These kids are part of me. I'm going to miss Jordan leaning back in his chair at the lunch table. I'm going to miss Aubrey's face, all grin and rabbit hair, after her morning pet feeding. There won't be anyone to string out all the dress-up clothes or dance around the house in my high-heeled shoes when Arianne's at school. I'm going to miss watching Joseph doctor his latest shriveled worm casualty on the driveway after a rainstorm. I'm going to miss being April's telephone-answering machine and picking T.P. out of the front yard trees after her sleep-over parties.

Sometimes my children seem like warts, annoying me and refusing to go away. But they've grown on me, and now, after all the days and nights that melt into years, they're part of me, and it hurts when they go away.

To Soar

There are still a few places where you can hear the wind wash through the pines and watch wild ducks take flight. Salem Pond is a quiet place where children can glide back and forth in old tire swings and watch earth, water, and sky gently meet in one clear reflection before their eyes.

The day had just begun to melt into night when we arrived. It was the hour of softness between light and darkness.

"Oh, look," my daughter April said, pointing to the wild ducks on the water. "They are so beautiful. Watch that one there. He glides just above the water before he sails away."

April was eleven, just weeks away from her twelfth birthday. She is like the month she was named for, fresh and full of life. She darted from the car and ran toward the ducks alongside the calm water.

The wild birds, not as sure of her gentleness, fled before her.

"Oh, Momma, they're frightened," she said. "I just want to hold them."

"Sometimes," I answered, "you have to sit quietly and wait for them to feel safe. Then they come to you."

April sat quietly at the edge of the water and waited. The birds watched her, and in time they approached cautiously. She extended her hand. They stepped back.

When she rose, they retreated back to the water and, with the expanse of wings, took flight. "They are so beautiful," April said, standing next to me. She noticed some young boys on the other side of the pond with BB guns. "What if they hurt them? I would love to take one home and tend it and feed it and keep it safe."

April walked away from me toward another group of wild birds lacing their way through the cattails. I noticed that her once childlike body was now slowly taking on the form of a woman. Though she was unaware, I knew that she too had begun her ascent; and some day in the too-near future, I would stand quietly at the edge of time and watch her take flight.

April slowly knelt and reached out to take possession, but the wild birds swam out of her reach. I watched her follow the animals with her eyes as they stretched their wings and soared.

"Will you help me catch one?" she asked. "I could take it home and keep it safe."

"It would be safe," I answered, "but it wouldn't be free."

"I think," April said after a long moment of silence, "wild birds shouldn't be pets. I think I can love them best from here on the shore."

Household Helpers I Have Not Known

Being a homemaker is sometimes the loneliest occupation on earth. You may be sitting there with twenty-seven happy, crazy people having fun throwing paper airplanes, popcorn, and darts, while eating pizza and green olives, but as soon as you suggest, "Hey, why don't we clean up," everyone suddenly dissolves into thin air.

It wasn't always like this. When my children were young, they were always following me around begging to be allowed to vacuum, dust, and clean. But after they were old enough to be any real help, the offers stopped and never came again.

Now that my children are old enough to really help, they don't see any point to it. Whenever I say, "Why don't you make your bed before you leave," they answer, "But, Mom, I'm just going to crawl back into it and mess it all up again in a few hours anyway."

When I finally get them to make their beds, I ask, "Why do you make your bed up and over your clean clothes, dear?"

They each say, "Well, Mom, you're the one who keeps putting all those clean clothes on the bottom of my bed. What else do you expect me to do?"

They say, "You always want everything so perfect, Mom. Well, I like a little mess. What's more, I like a lot of mess."

I say, "All I want is a clear path through the clutter so I won't trip and fall on my face."

"Well it's your fault," they chide me. "You're the one who always wanted a big family."

When my children finally reach the age when I've trained them to be built-in babysitters, they always have better-paying jobs elsewhere. I could go somewhere, anywhere, without half a dozen small children velcroed to my arms and legs. But of course my older children have a waiting list of paying customers for babysitting jobs, and I'm way down on the list waiting my turn, because I make them work without paying them a measly dime.

My adolescent children remind me of the Blob. The Blob is a large glob of near-motionless matter used in the old movies to scare unsuspecting adults when they had their backs turned.

When I ask, "Have you done your homework, made your bed, or practiced the piano?" there is no response. They sit in the chair and become the Blob, an expressionless, emotionless glob. I'm afraid to kick it and see if it's still alive for fear it will ooze over to me and suck me into oblivion.

But there are other times—times when I hear the piano actually being played without promise of reward or punishment, times when someone says, "What can I do to help you, Mom?"

Every once in a while I see a wet towel hung up or a smelly sock in the hamper without my assistance. After I check a few foreheads for fever, I'm in love again.

A childless couple recently invited our family up to their cabin for a few days. Vale, our hostess, was scrubbing, baking, stirring, slicing, or serving food to us at all hours. I worried about the extra work we were creating and tried to help the best could. I apologized over and over again.

"Oh," she answered, "don't apologize, please. This is so satisfying for me. You see, I don't have the opportunity of cooking and cleaning for a family. It feels good."

Gratifying? I thought. Opportunity?

I usually felt like a food factory. It never occurred to me that what I was doing could be gratifying. In the simple act of cooking a meal for my family, I was, in reality, "feeding the hungry."

It never occurred to me that sewing, shopping, or washing my children's smelly gym clothes could be "clothing the naked." I never thought rocking my green-faced child or washing her bedding after the stomach flu was part of "healing the sick." Something about Vale told me she understood these things, she missed doing these things.

Being a homemaker may be lonely at times, but at other times it can be the most gratifying career on earth.

Scouting School

When the bishop's counselor summoned me into the office, he put his heavy arm on my sagging shoulder and asked, "Sister Baadsgaard, will you be a den mother for the Bobcats?"

Oh, great! Now the ward is trying to round up volunteers to put some time in down at the zoo, I thought. Brother Beebe motioned for me to sit down in the chair opposite him.

I squirmed in my seat and replied, "But, Brother Beebe, I'm already going under with my little monkeys at home."

"Don't worry," the counselor said. "They aren't Bobcats for long. Then they become Wolves. You're supposed to have den meetings in your home every week, and pack night every month with the Bears."

"This is ridiculous," I answered. "I won't even let my kids bring home stray cats or dogs."

"No, the Bobcats and Wolves are boys, Sister Baadsgaard," he replied.

"You mean boys who act like animals?" I asked.

"You could put it that way," he answered. "This is Scouting, Sister Baadsgaard. You know, 'On my honor . . .'" he finished, making a gesture with his fingers.

"I'm from a family of eight girls," I answered. "And my mother taught us never to swear or make gestures with our fingers."

"Sister Baadsgaard, I'm sure you'll do just fine. Trust me. There's nothing to it."

Those were his final words as he shoved a pile of books, charts, and posters at me, then smiled as he pushed me out of the door.

"Wow," I thought after reading all the material I could find to educate myself. "This is the only organization I know of that demands you pay them money to have the privilege of donating your time as a leader volunteer. They must have something good hidden in here somewhere."

I didn't do very well in my first leadership planning meeting. When the council leader said, "Our pack will be lashing teepees at the jamboree in the North Park," I thought they meant T.P.

Maybe this is the Scouting way to prepare a 72-hour emergency kit, I thought. When the other leaders noticed my puzzled expression they asked me if I had a problem with that.

"Well, I guess not," I replied, "but what on earth do you want to do with a bunch of toilet paper lashed together?"

Learning all the terms that go with Scouting is like learning a foreign language. Words like *Akela* and *Webelos* may look like English, but they're really Cub Scoutese.

Just when I was ready to hand in my resignation, something happened to change my mind. After all my struggling with terms and leadership meetings, I finally held the first den meeting at my home. Eleven eight-year-old boys hesitantly knocked on my front door. Most of them forgot their Wolf book and dues, and a good share forgot their manners and their front teeth. But they all brought these wide-open eyes and fresh faces as they looked up to me.

I couldn't help myself. I fell in love—not so much with Scouting as with Willy, Jordan, John, Michael, Matt, Cody, and all the rest. We talked through tin cans connected with string, raced Matchbox cars, ate chocolate chip cookies, and learned to clamp our jaws when Akela threw two fingers in the air.

I never learned to speak Scouting fluently before they released me and assigned me to work in the Young Women's program, but whenever I see "my" boys now, I know Scouting is about more than canteens and registration money. It's about toothless, wide-eyed boys and overly sentimental, uneducated den mothers who just can't help themselves.

Shopping on a Shoestring Can Trip You

There are three words the rich and famous among us will never hear: "Attention, Kmart shoppers!"

But the rest of us who have to live on a budget know why shopping on a shoestring can trip you.

Take, for instance, the plight of the local Kmart shoe shoppers. These men, women, and children, rendered immobile with retail pricing techniques, deserve a medal. Once you try on a pair of shoes at this store, you're in for a major decision with unknown consequences.

All Kmart shoes come hooked together with a very strong plastic string. If the shopper wants to see how the shoes feel when he walks in them, he can either waddle down the aisle a quarter inch at a time or peer over his shoulder while he cuts the plastic string with his teeth.

The first time I tried on a pair of Kmart shoes, I left the plastic string intact and waddled. It was impossible to look even slightly intelligent while I shuffled about the store in what was the equivalent of having my shoelaces tied together.

The next time I tried on a pair of shoes, I tried to bite them apart, but ended up with a horrendous dentist bill instead. Next I tried fingernail clippers and nail files. After each attempt I was sweating profusely, not so much from the effort as from the fear of being caught by store security. They probably send people like me to the same place they send people who tear the tags off pillows.

All this brings us, of course, to the larger issue of price tag stems. How do retailers get those plastic things through the clothing we buy, anyway? If you try pulling them out, they make a terrible hole. And those few retailers who don't use plastic stems with fat things on both ends use paper price tags attached with Super Glue.

They say ice cream cones were invented by a soda shop lad who hated doing dishes. Now, if one of us budget buyers would just invent edible price tags.

The greatest discoveries are yet to be made. Jake Page, an editorial consultant for the Smithsonian's National Air and Space Museum, may be on the brink of answering the greatest mystery of all: Where do all the sock mates go? He noted that wire coat hangers, when left alone, tangle themselves up and reproduce. He's always wanted to know where socks go, and it suddenly came to him: socks are the larval form of wire coat hangers.

If editorial consultants for the Smithsonian's National Air and Space Museum can make important observations like that, just imagine what the rest of us can come up with—that is, of course, unless we listen to the experts.

Charles H. Duell, director of the U.S. Patent Office in 1899, said very authoritatively, "Everything that can be invented has been invented."

Robert Millikan, who won a Nobel Prize in physics, told us our limits when he said, "There is no likelihood man can ever tap the power of the atom."

Grover Cleveland told women how to be more sensible and responsible when he told us, "Sensible and responsible women do not want to vote."

Harry M. Warner of Warner Brothers Pictures in 1927 certainly knew what the moviegoing public really wanted when he said, "Who wants to hear actors talk?"

Somewhere out there in some humble kitchen is a woman who will discover the ultimate answer to life's greatest mystery: how to babyproof your home without throwing out the baby. So hang in there, budget buyers. Dreams don't cost a cent.

Summer Breakdown

I heard some parenting expert on the radio the other day tell me to give my kids and myself two or three weeks to adjust to the new summertime routine. She said she thoroughly enjoyed having her kids home during the summer and hated the new year-round school schedule.

"Children really need a summer break," she finished.

She was right about one thing. Children do break in the summer. They break their legs, each other's faces, the dining room table, and their mother's nervous system. It's a circus at my house in the summer. I give my family a few weeks to adjust to the new freedom, and frankly, things generally get progressively worse, not better.

Summer break always finds me wishing I could have a nervous breakdown. Each year I contemplate sitting calmly in our overstuffed armchair letting all my nerves blow and smoke one at a time while I go comatose, mumbling, "Get me to the state hospital. I'm going crazy." But I'm afraid nobody would even notice, and I'd have to get up and go to the bathroom eventually.

I've been planning to have a nervous breakdown every summer for years. But every time I get ready to have one, I have to get up and fix supper. I don't know why I continue fixing food around here. My children never remember what they ate, even two minutes after they're through wolfing it down.

Even if my kids have only one or two friends over to the house apiece during the long, hot days of summer, that means about twenty-seven strange children of various ages, sizes, and manners wandering aimlessly around my small one-level house, following me into my bedroom and asking exactly the same question, "What can we do?"

If I close and lock the door for a little privacy, they pound and yell at me as though I were sitting under the chestnut tree on the next block. If that fails to get a response, they plop on their tummies, peek under the door, and send me handwritten messages through the crack.

My children ask such things as, "Mom, can I go play outside?" What they really mean is, "Can I go roll in the dirt, pick a fight with the neighbor's kids, get my head stuck in the ditch under the driveway, rip shingles off the shed roof, and light firecrackers in the garbage can?"

Why do I say yes?

My children politely ask, "Can we have a snack?" What they really mean is, "Can I smear peanut butter across the countertop, cabinets, floor, and through my hair, totally missing the piece of bread, while I spill my glass of milk?"

Why do I say yes?

"You always say no," my son says as the day wears on and I've finally learned my lesson. "If Dad were home, I bet he'd say yes. He's nicer than you."

"Oh, yeah?" I answer. "Well, your dad doesn't live here. He just comes home for a few hours after work, and even then he hides out in the bathroom with the newspaper. He doesn't *live* here. Now, tell me, son, what is it about the word 'no' that you do not understand!"

Truly, there is nothing so rare as a peaceful day during summer break.

CHAPTER 6

FAMILY HISTORY

THE AGE OF REASON
GOLDEN PERIOD

When man and wife their love entwine,
Reproduction's next in line.
One plus one makes three, you see.
We're a happy family?
Families may be really fine,
But no one ever toes the line.
Little brother plays the goon,
The rest of us sing out of tune.
Families make the human race,
But we have trouble saving face.
Families aren't a rarity—
Just look back to your ancestry,
And now . . . to your posterity.

The Bread and Milk of Living

Being able to fast on the first Sunday of every month is the unspoken rite of passage in many Mormon families—the bridge between childhood and mature adulthood.

When I was growing up, the children in my family had to somehow convince my parents of their ripening maturity before Mom and Dad would pass on the privilege and honor of partaking of the spiritual feast that fasting provides.

I'd been looking forward to this honor for months. I had finally convinced my parents I was ready to make that sacrifice along with all the other mature members of my family. I didn't know going without food would teach me about the bread and milk of living.

When that long-anticipated fast day came, I watched my younger sisters hawklike while they gobbled up their toast, eggs, and milk. In my sanctimonious sanctuary on the couch, as I watched each one finish her last bite, I began to seriously wonder why I had begged for this privilege.

That day, after long hours in church, I kept looking at the clock. Morning grew into afternoon, and I was still holding firm to my commitment. Then I remembered I had half a roll of Lifesavers in my coat pocket. I figured I could sneak them out and carry them down to the bathroom, close the door, and lock it. If I flushed the toilet while I rattled the paper, nobody would be able to hear me eating the candy.

I grabbed the Lifesavers from my coat pocket, hid them in my dress pocket, and walked downstairs to the bathroom. Then I closed the door, flushed the toilet, and ripped open the paper. As I sat down on the heat vent, ready to eat it, I stared at the cherry Lifesaver between my thumb and index finger, about three inches from my mouth.

Then guilt hit. I took the candy, flushed it down the toilet, then walked outside the house and waited.

When Mom called me to dinner from the house, it didn't take me long to slide into my place at the table. My mother and father smiled at me and patted me on the arm.

I looked at the table, which held a loaf of sliced bread, a gallon pitcher of chilled milk, and slices of cheese stacked on a china plate. Every Sunday night our family had bread and milk for supper. We would take a slice of bread, break it into small pieces in a bowl, pour milk over it, and eat the mixture with a spoon.

As I took my slice of bread and slowly broke it into the bowl, I could feel the smooth, soft texture of the bread center and the hard, shiny dark brown crust. I noticed the moisture from the chilled milk running down the side of the glass. As I poured the milk into the bowl, it made a frothy top.

It was a simple meal, an ordinary meal, a meal we had eaten every Sunday night for as long as I could remember. But it tasted different that night. I distinctly remember the yeasty smell of the bread and the way the cool milk felt inside my mouth. I've never had a meal quite like it since.

That meal taught me about the bread and milk of living, about the richness of ordinary things. I found that really enjoying life could be as simple as being able to savor an ordinary meal.

Now I am the mother who quietly watches my children discover the law of the fast. I've heard them self-righteously intimidate their younger brothers and sisters who are too young to fast. I have heard them desperately plead for me to start dinner early. I've seen them struggle with a growling stomach and a light head. I've seen them grow progressively more and more cross and irritable.

I've also seen their quiet faces when we say our family "fast" prayer to close our fast together. I've seen their hungry fingers grab, then suddenly become more gentle when they touch the first slice of bread. I've seen them savor a meal like never before.

I hope they discover that the real bread and milk of our lives is knowing it isn't the big things that need our closest attention. It is the simple meals, the ordinary events, that need our careful observation and appreciation. It is the depth, not the breadth, that really matters. It's knowing that even a simple meal of bread and milk is fit for a king.

The real bread and milk of life is knowing there is more than one way to feed ourselves. It's knowing that each moment of our lives, as common as it may seem, needs to be valued and relished. It's knowing we need to pause between the chapters or days of our lives to ponder and give it all meaning.

The Bitter and the Sweet

"I brought you some peaches," she said when I answered the front door. "I don't do much canning any more, now that there's only me to do for. I thought your family could use these. They're clingstone, but they taste good."

I took the peaches and ushered her through the door toward the kitchen. After I'd transferred the peaches into my own bowl, I slipped the empty bowl back into her hands and thanked her.

'How've you been doing?" she asked, making herself comfortable in a chair next to the kitchen table. "I've been thinking about you lately and getting a bit lonely to talk to you. I see you at church, but that doesn't seem good enough."

"I'm fine," I answered. "I felt the baby move yesterday. The doctor says everything looks good this time. We have our fingers crossed."

School had recently started, canning season was in full swing, my church responsibilities had taken extra time lately, and I hadn't even noticed it had been weeks since we'd talked together. Now that I could relax and think about it, I'd missed her too. I sat down opposite her at the table and took a breather from folding clothes, washing dishes, and chasing my preschoolers around the house after they had painted each other's bellies with oil paint. It felt good to be near her, my eighty-six-year-old neighbor and good friend, Edna Gerber.

She'd been through these growing years with me. Whenever things got a little crazy and I thought I might blow my top at the children, I'd always suggest they go visit Mrs. Gerber. They always came back with a grin and a piece of candy drooling down their chins.

With a few minutes of quiet to myself, I could handle the rest of the day after they returned. She had rescued me many, many times over the years. I doubted she knew that.

"How've you been?" I asked. "How's your hernia? Does it still get you up at night?"

"It's not too bad," she said. "The doctor said the risks of surgery at my age would be greater than just enduring the pain. It gets me up at night, but I take something warm, turn on the radio, and I can usually get back to sleep. But I feel so guilty because I sleep in until eight o'clock and don't seem to be able to get as much done as I'd like."

Edna's hair is soft and gray, her skin wrinkled and smooth. She wears thick glasses that help with her failing eyesight and a hearing aid to help with advancing deafness.

"But you know, everybody has something bothering them or paining them," Edna continued. "This is just mine. I used to think life would be so easy when I got my family all raised, that all my troubles would be pretty much over. But I've discovered problems don't go away—they just change. I think a person's only happy if they live happily even with troubles and pain, knowing there's no easy time of life. Life's full of good and bad, but it's knowing a few hard times that makes the good times seem so sweet."

That night, my growing family shared the peaches she had brought over. As the sweetness lingered on my tongue, I looked round the table at my children, smiled contentedly, and took a deep breath.

"Pass the milk," my eight-year-old yelled across the table. "Can't you hear me? You deaf?"

"Mom, tell Joseph to quit kicking me," Arianne insisted. Someone spilled their milk, and someone flipped their peas across the table with their fork while the three-year-old stood up in his chair, tumbled backward, and banged his head on the floor.

Amid the screams I heard the words again: Problems don't go away—they just change. But it's knowing a few hard times that makes the good times seem so sweet.

I hurried for a cold wash rag to soothe a bruised head.

Even after the children were herded out of the kitchen and the dish washing was done, the sweet scent of Edna's peaches still filled the room.

I Will Wait for Spring

She was carrying hot turkey soup and chocolate-striped cookies on a china plate when she knocked at my door. "How are you feeling?" she asked. "I've brought some warm soup for your lunch."

She walked into my kitchen and set the homemade soup and cookies on the counter. Then she turned to me.

"I'm so sorry," she said. "When something bad happens to someone you love, you feel like you're going through it with him."

She hugged me. I could feel the soft fur collar on her coat and the warmth of her cheek against mine.

"I love you," she whispered in my ear.

We walked slowly toward the door.

"I was going to ask you," she continued. "Is a miscarriage like having a baby, with the pain and all?"

Then it all came flooding back. The past month in and out of bed with spotting, cramping, and uncertainty. Then there was the sudden hemorrhage, the hurried call to the doctor, the rushed trip to the emergency room, the stirrups, IV, blood, nausea, contractions, the doctor too busy watching a basketball game to come in time, the nurse carrying warm blankets, the worried husband with his firm palm on my moist forehead.

"Yes," I answered. "It's like having a baby. It *is* having a baby . . . too soon."

My husband took off his coat to keep me warm on the drive home from the emergency room that black February night. He cradled my head in his lap, his arms shaking with the cold. When we arrived home, he carried me from the car to the bedroom, quietly closed the door, and tried to explain to our other children what had happened.

The next day, when I wanted to belt the doctor who wouldn't leave the basketball game, scream at my other children for still needing to be fed, and tear the wash that still needed to be done, my husband took me in his arms until the shaking and sobbing eased. Then he fixed supper for the children and took care of the mountain of washing.

"Mommy?" my four-year-old son, Joseph, asked me later that night. "Did our baby die?"

"Yes, honey," I answered.

"But you were supposed to take your vitamins so our baby wouldn't die," Joseph said.

"I did take my vitamins," I answered. "But our baby died anyway."

"I wanted our baby to be a boy so I could play with him in the backyard," Joseph said.

"I know, honey," I answered. "I wanted our baby too."

Joseph pulled his eyebrows together and thought for a long time.

"Maybe Heavenly Father will save another baby for us," Joseph said, his face brightening.

"I hope so, Joseph," I answered. "I hope so."

Weeks later, an ache in my center lingered, a feeling there was no inside of me. Snow was falling that morning. I hadn't been out of the safe, warm cocoon of my home since it happened. It seemed wrong of the world to just keep going along with all the usual things. I wanted everything and everyone to stop for a moment and let me say good-bye. But there were still carpet cleaning salesmen on the telephone, dishes to wash, and garbage cans to be brought in from the street.

It was cold outside, cold and threatening. I forced myself to push my feet inside my boots and trudge out to the street. I grabbed a smashed garbage can in each hand, then headed for the gate of the fence enclosing our backyard.

Swinging the gate wide, I sidestepped through the opening to the backyard, kicking the gate closed behind me. The snow lay unsoiled and untouched before me, changing everything to something new, clean, and white.

I walked slowly to the back of the house, dragging the cans at my sides. The sun was setting and gave the snow a warm glow. An icicle, hanging precariously from the roof, broke off and shattered like broken glass on the snow crust below. The air was hushed and silent.

I caught my breath and held it. My eyes stung. For the first me in a long while, I was able to look at the world in awe, overcome with the beauty around me.

A sense of reverence swept over me as I walked where no one had walked before. The sun slowly sank lower in the western sky, and I saw the color of the snow change from a warm, golden glow to a clear, cool blue.

The new year was upon me with all the unknown way I had go. But I knew I had to say good-bye before I could say hello. I imagined the gentle earth lying beneath the drifts of snow, submissive to the trust the seasons keep. I felt reborn to the miracle of the cycle of loss and gain, darkness and light, life and death.

"Good-bye," I whispered in the stillness. "I will wait for spring."

Love Lines

Sometimes being family has more to do with love lines than blood lines.

GOLDEN PERIOD

I remember feeling burdened when the Relief Society president asked me to look in on a woman on my visiting teaching district. I had already made my monthly visit to her, my children were all ill at the time, and I was tired and worn out from lack of sleep. I went out of duty—certainly not out of compassion.

On the way to the woman's house, I figured that because she was childless, she didn't realize how easy her life was. *She always exaggerates her illnesses,* I thought judgmentally. *If she had a family to take care of, she wouldn't have the luxury of staying in bed and feeling sorry for herself.*

When I walked into the house, I could hear the woman moaning in her bedroom. I didn't feel much sympathy. I looked for something to clean, but her house was spotless. I went into the kitchen to fix a meal, but the refrigerator was already bulging with food brought in by other ward members.

I finally walked into the woman's bedroom and sat down at the side of her bed. She immediately turned toward me and began detailing a long list of aches and pains. I listened impatiently at first, but as she continued to talk, my mind let go of judging her. This woman was well off financially. Her late husband had left her secure. She seemed to have few needs. But it suddenly occurred to me that it had probably been a very long time since anyone had touched this woman. Sometimes we realize that people need more than casseroles.

"Would you like a foot rub?" I asked.

"A what?" she responded.

"A foot rub. My mother says a foot rub can do a sick body wonders."

I pushed aside the blankets, picked up her small foot, and laid it gently in my lap. It was cold and stiff at first, but as I rubbed my thumbs in a circular motion on the arch of her foot, her tense muscles relaxed one by one. When I finished several minutes later, the woman looked up into my eyes. She touched my hand with hers and quietly said, "Thank you."

I felt a new appreciation for this woman's circumstances.

Although they were different from my own, they were equally challenging. She had no bright faces to wake her in the morning. She had never had her own baby to rock and cradle in her arms, and she was my sister.

In our hectic modern existence and with the many demands on our time and compassion, we sometimes feel like part of a large orchestra warming up before the concert begins. Each individual's instrument or act of kindness sometimes seems disjointed, out of harmony. But learning to love as the Savior loves is the most important thing we can learn in this life.

When the Master steps forward, only his musicians' eyes are upon him. And when he raises his hands, they will see the prints of the nails in his palms. Then they begin to understand: all the practicing and warming up have prepared them for this moment when they can begin the music of their finest hour. This music, powerful and unified by their compassion, grows from pianissimo to fortissimo, filling the world with a symphony of love.

"And the King shall answer and say unto them, Verily I say to you, Inasmuch as ye have done it unto one of the least of these my brethren, ye have done it unto me" (Matt. 25:40).

No Degree, Position, or Possession

Last week my husband and I were checking out our overflowing grocery cart at a local warehouse food store.

While the checker was ringing up our twelve gallons of milk, she asked, "How many children do you have?"

"Ten," we answered.

"Boy, I feel sorry for you," the checker said, shaking her head. Then she looked us over. "But you guys don't look like you have ten children. You look ... well ... you look good. I can usually tell just by looking how many children a couple has."

The checker was young and pretty and seemed to hold the stereotyped image held by most members of our society: people who have more than one or two children are either members of certain religious or ethnic groups, live on welfare, or are not very fast learners.

I have a different opinion. I think families are "it." Everything else is extra baggage. Families are the glue that holds the world together, because we are all brothers and sisters.

I've been writing about the joys and frustrations of families for many years now. From some publications I've received less-than-friendly letters containing explicit instructions on which form of birth control I should be using or copies of magazine articles that claim large families deplete natural resources and stymie conservation efforts. I've also received letters from parents who are raising children and feel they are doing something rather important.

I've been raised in a generation that took the bait— hook, line, and sinker. Many of us actually believed having children is mildly selfish at best and that producing more than two per family would be an act of pollution.

With the increased availability of contraception and abortion, coupled with economic and social pressures, couples in many countries are producing later and smaller families.

Today's world seems to have lost its wonder at the miracle of life. Birth and human growth and fulfillment with age seem to have become more an interruption of life than the true object. We need a reacceptance that the family is the end, not the means. The family is the race, not the pit stop.

No, all families are definitely not perfect. Families have problems. All families have problems. I've been involved with diapers for thirty years, and there are times when I wonder if it's all worth it. Some days the confusion and the fighting are enough to make me wish for a one-way ticket to a lonely island somewhere in the Pacific. But then I remember my children's faces when I check on them in their beds at night.

A while back I graduated from BYU. It was the conclusion of a family project with which everybody had to help out. When

I walked out of the auditorium in my cap and gown, all my children, dressed in their Sunday best, raced into my arms. Their father soon followed and joined in the mass embrace.

While we were taking pictures on the lawn, a group of people gathered and watched. "You have a very special family," one middle-aged woman said while she watched.

For me, no degree, position, or possession can replace that.

Family Portrait

A polite gentleman at the big city newspaper called a while back and asked, "Mrs. Baadsgaard, would it be possible for you to bring in your family to the editorial offices of the paper? We'd like a picture of you and your family to run sometime between now and Mother's Day."

Only a fellow mother could possibly know what fear and trembling that question produced. You see, asking a mother if she would like her family portrait taken is like asking her if she would like to have her ears slowly twisted off her head.

"Sure, we'd love to," I lied. "Just set the time, and we'll be there."

The first thing I had to do was convince my whole crew of nonconformers that dressing up in their Sunday clothes when it wasn't Sunday would not permanently damage their health or their happy childhood memories.

"Why do we have to wear our yucky clothes?"

"I'm not getting dressed up on Wednesday."

"Why do I have to wear my church pants? The holes in my jeans aren't that big."

"I'll keep my arm down so nobody will see the rip in the armpit if you let me wear my Garfield T-shirt."

"I'm not wearing a tie. No way."

"I hate this sweater. It makes my armpits itch."

"I'm not going to wear those shoes. They make my toes quashed."

"I'm not going to wear this dress. The lace makes my neck break out in a rash."

"No, I don't know where the mate to my other Sunday shoe is. The last time I saw it, Bowdens' dog was burying it in the field across the street."

I've been known to utter unprintable threats at this point. My husband, wiser than I, was hiding out in the bathroom with the door locked, reading the sports section.

Boys were easier when it came to hair-fixing time. I simply dipped their heads under the faucet and started plastering. My girls, on the other hand, required more time and caused more frustration. By the time I got all the electric rollers, curling irons, and blow dryers in use, we started picking up radio signals. There are never enough rollers to go around, so we curled in shifts.

After we crammed into the car, the children counted off to make sure some forgotten child was not connected to a curling iron in the back bedroom in a valiant effort to get left behind.

Then came the tricky part: the hour-long drive to the newspaper office. All my male children have an odd addiction to in-car head bouncing. (My mother-in-law said they inherited it from their father, who spent his entire first year of life banging his head on his crib slats.) These dear male children sat up straight in the car, throwing their heads backward, which caused their loosely packed brains to ricochet off the bench seat behind them until their eyes glazed over and their tongues dropped out.

While they bounced back and forth, my boys yell-hummed "Book of Mormon Stories" in a monotone buzz. It wasn't long until the static electricity they produced made every shaft of hair in the car stick straight out like a dandelion gone to seed. The other male in the car, who happened to be driving, was fast reaching a countdown to explosion as even his nostrils flared.

The girls in the car promptly stuck their heads out of the window like dogs, panting and yelling "Too hot!" The girls who didn't follow this procedure sweated every last bit of curl out of their heads in seven minutes flat. What we had now was a carful of boys with static-puffed hair and girls with limp or ratty wind-blown hair.

About this time, some sneaky child pulled chocolate candy out of his pocket and started passing it around. I, of course, didn't notice a thing until we arrived at our point of destination and I found my children all had brown faces and spotted clothes.

By the time we piled out of the car, all undershirts were sticking out, zippers had flown open, collars were unbuttoned down to the navel, leotards were bagging around the ankles, and all the hair bows had been lost somewhere under the car seats.

Getting the kids all into the door of the newspaper office, up the stairs, through the newsroom, and into the photo lab was like trying to herd a bunch of ants back down the hole in the anthill. When the photographer finally lined the family up for the picture, he was sweating as profusely as I was.

"Look this way. No. No. No. Over here. Watch the birdie. Hey, kids! Look at me. Bzzzzzzzz [long, loud, obnoxious sound made with tongue between the lips.] Now, children. No, don't put your fingers ... would someone turn that child's head? No, open your eyes and close your mouth. Put your ..."

All too late came a series of clicks and several flashes of light. There we were, an honest-to-goodness, real rough-draft family, suspended for a moment in time.

On the final print, Joseph had his mouth covered with both hands. Jacob's eyes were half shut and his finger was up his nose. Arianne had her lips sucked inside her teeth. Jordan used two fingers to make horns on his mother. Aubrey was staring aimlessly off into space with a meaningless expression. April had her cheeks pushed out, her tongue protruding, and her ears fanned forward in her famous monkey imitation. My husband wore a totally baffled expression. I was smiling with a clenched jaw as the baby used my finger for a teething ring. There wasn't much that even a good touch-up artist could do to rescue this negative.

Later we piled back into the car and headed for home. In two seconds flat, all neck-pinching ties disappeared, shirttails flew out, and baggy leotards and squishy shoes found themselves crammed under the back seat. Even my torso-squeezing panty hose took up residence in the glove compartment.

When we hit the freeway, the back seat grew quiet. When I turned around to see what everybody was up to, I saw Jacob's sleepy head balanced on April's shoulder, Joseph's drowsy head cradled in Jordan's lap, and Aubrey and Arianne curled like spoons in a drawer, fast asleep in the cargo area. The baby had fallen asleep in her car seat with her head wedged against two wrinkled Sunday shirts, and she was sucking her thumb. I motioned for Ross to look in his rearview mirror. We turned and looked into each other's eyes at the same moment as our whole bodies relaxed into smiles.

There was no photographer in the car to take a picture now, shutter to click or lights to flash. But I took my own private picture and tucked it away in the memory album of my heart. I'm still attempting the massive work of our family saga. But in truth, I love this rough draft stage. That's where all the joy of creation and the pain of revision comes in. Anything is possible as long as I don't come due for grading next week.

You see, I don't believe true happiness will be found in the acquisition of things or the rise to position. I don't believe happiness will be found in faraway places with exotic names. I believe true happiness will ultimately be found at home. Our family portrait on the mantel may be a little flawed, but it's real. And the best family portraits can't be hung on the wall or framed on shelf.

Call it a network if you will, a community, kinsmen, clan, or family. Whatever you call it, we all need one. Before we were born, all around us now, and after we die, there are others who need to matter a great deal to us. Even if some who live alone choose solitude by election, none of us lives fully without each other. In a world at peace, a soul at peace, we will all be important to one another.

It matters little if our present dwelling houses a family of one or of thirteen. For when we truly come home, we discover the family of man—the universal brotherhood and sisterhood of us all. When we come home to our true selves, we need never leave again.

After a particularly exasperating evening that was filled with repeated attempts to get my jack-in-the-box child to sleep, I tucked my four-year-old son, Jacob, into bed one more time with an irritated sigh.

"What am I going to do with you, Jacob?" I asked.

He didn't even hesitate before he answered, "Oh, Mommy. Just hug me, and pretty soon I'll grow up."

After all the years of patience, energy, and tummy stretching beyond any reasonable expectations, I often feel that I should resign. I am simply not what I think a mother should be. Too many times I'm grumpy when I should be understanding, cross when I should be gentle, preoccupied when I should be attentive. But I've found that in spite of my incompetence, in spite of my obvious lack of skill, my children still love me.

Sometimes I wonder if after a long day my children wish they could put me to bed with a sigh: "Oh, Mom, what are we going to do with you?"

In my heart I answer, "Just hug me, and pretty soon I'll grow up."

In the End

The close of a year is a perfect time for a little philosophical melancholy. As I watch the last weathered leaves fall from trees and feel frost steal life from gardens and flowers, I realize time is passing and here I am ... still as dumb as I ever was.

I used to watch wise veteran mothers react to their children's antics. Missy and Bozo could be spinning cartwheels off the ceiling rafters, and wise, wonderful Mother would just sit there with

GOLDEN PERIOD

a serene smile on her face. When my kids tried any hair-raising feats of daring or stupidity, I routinely threw a ninny fit and yelled at them to get down from there before they fell and broke their necks or gave me a heart attack.

Someday, I kept telling myself, I'll be one of those serene, white-haired mothers who smiled a lot and who never yelled or lost their tempers.

I say that because something weird happened the other day. One of my kids was gouging the sofa upholstery, another was gouging his brother, another had her radio turned up enough to cause sudden hair loss, another yelled that the toilet was overflowing, the telephone rang, and the baby started choking on something she had snarfed up under the dinner table while I chatted with the neighbor.

"Boy, you're sure a patient mother," my neighbor said, glaring at my overactive family while I casually continued our conversation.

Then I realized—I wasn't patient. I had a bad head cold and I was just too tired to get nervous, mad, or insane.

This experience has been troubling me. "What if?" I questioned myself. "What if all those mothers I thought were wise and serene simply had head colds or were just too dog tired?"

It kind of blows your image of the older generation when you start to become one of them and you know you're still as dumb as you ever were. Then I started thinking, "The more I keep thinking that I'll be better later, the less time I have to really get a kick out of today."

Most of us are pretty strange about this weighty business called living. For instance, the only time we really appreciate how it feels not to have a head cold is when we have one.

Maybe the secret is realizing we're not necessarily going to get a lot wiser or smarter. Maybe we're always going to be just our struggling selves. Maybe the trick is discovering that *that* self is incomparable, unique, and irreplaceable.

As Michelangelo has been quoted as saying, "I saw the angel

in the marble and I just chiseled till I set him free." Maybe the passing seasons will knock off a bit of rough stone here and there, and finally, if we get a whole bunch of knocks, we will come to find our true selves, that angel within who is waiting to be set free, that person who was just us, all along.

Rough Draft Families

As I sat around a table with several neighbor ladies at our last Relief Society social, I described how my "well-bred" children had discovered a new way to secure their favorite places at the table before other rival siblings could grab them.

"They spit on the plate," I said, my eyes rolling back in my head.

The lady sitting next to me gasped. "You mean your kids do things like that?"

"What? You thought they didn't?" I asked.

"Well, I didn't know," she answered. "I thought my kids were the only ones who did things like that. It just seems like your children are such perfect angels when they're at church."

"You must have been so busy trying to keep your own kids quiet that you just happened to look over at mine during the one and only seven-second interval when nobody was doing anything obnoxious," I answered.

Why is it we all let this edited version of other families throw us into a panic? The fact is, we're all untried authors at this family business. And I think our unedited versions are a lot more interesting. If you definitely feel a bit carsick at times trying to ride the ups and downs of family life, you have a lot of company. My own family is definitely not a group of angels. (The children take after their father, of course.)

In the past when I looked at all the edited mothers in church or at the store, dressed up, smiling, and polite, I really believed they always looked and acted like that. I was positive I was the only mother with hair that stands straight up when I wake up in the morning, the only one who wears fuzzy slippers, the only one who laughs like a lovesick hyena.

I thought I was the only mother in the world whose physical fitness program consisted of jumping to conclusions, flying off the handle, running up the electric bill, dodging my responsibility, and pushing my luck. But I don't believe that I'm alone anymore.

You know, motherhood is no piece of cake. Being a mother constantly requires you to act a little more mature and intelligent than the children, when in reality you know you're learning a lot more from your kids than they're learning from you.

I have to admit, there have been days when I've seriously wondered why Jesus would liken the kingdom of God to a child. But every night before I retire, I know. No matter how completely my offspring have destroyed my possessions, pride, or sense of humor during the day, when I take my nightly walk to check on my sleeping children, all is forgiven. In those quiet late-night moments a swelling rises, and I long to cradle each child in my arms, even those far larger than myself, and rock them back and forth.

Then life goes on, and children grow up; and soon, somewhere out there in the darkness, my child will be rocking his child, who someday will rock his child, and the cycle will continue without completion in one magnificent whole.

I love being part of all this!

About the Author

Janene Wolsey Baadsgaard has written extensively with warmth and humor about family life for over twenty-five years. She is the author of ten books as well as hundreds of newspaper columns, features, magazine articles. As a mother of ten children, she definitely knows first-hand about the perils and pleasures of motherhood. She is a graduate of Brigham Young University in Communications and has taught English and literature courses for Utah Valley State College. She is a full-time homemaker and lives on two acres in the country between Spanish Fork and Mapleton, Utah.

Janene enjoys four-wheeling in the mountains that surround her home. She says she used to ride on the back of the four-wheeler while her husband Ross drove . . . but he was always riding through wet cow pies that flipped up her back and landed on top of her head. She now drives her own four-wheeler.

Some of her other book titles include: *Is There Life After Birth?*, *A Sense of Wonder*, *Why Does My Mother's Day Potted Plant Always Die?*, *Families Who Laugh . . . Last*, *Family Finances For the Flabbergasted*, *Grin and Share It . . . Raising A Family With a Sense of Humor*, *Sister Bishop's Christmas Miracle*, *Expecting Joy* and *The LDS Mother's Almanac*.